CHRISTOS YANNARAS
POSTMODERN METAPHYSICS

CHRISTOS YANNARAS

POSTMODERN METAPHYSICS

Translated
by
Norman Russell

HOLY CROSS ORTHODOX PRESS
Brookline, Massachusetts

Original Title in Greek: *Meta-neôterikê meta-physikê.*
Published in Athens in 1993.

Published by Holy Cross Orthodox Press
50 Goddard Avenue
Brookline, Massachusetts 02445

On the cover: Giorgio de Chirico (1888-1978), *L'énigme de la fatalité*, 1914, oil painting, Emmanuel Hoffman-Stiftung/Kunstmuseum Basel, Switzerland. © 2004 Artists Rights Society (ARS), New York / SIAE, Rome.

ISBN 1-885652-80-1

LIBRARY OF CONGRESS CATALOGING–IN–PUBLICATION DATA

Giannaras, Chråestos, 1935-
[Meta-neåoterikåe, meta-physikåe. English]
Postmodern metaphysics / Christos Yannaras ; translated by Norman Russell.
p. cm.
Includes bibliographical references and indexes.
ISBN 1-885652-80-1 (pbk. : alk. paper)
1. Postmodernism. 2. Philosophy, Modern. I. Title.
B831.2.G5313 2005
110–dc22 2004022789

CONTENTS

Prolegomena 1

The Modern Paradigm

1. Historical context

European historiography takes the fall of Constantinople (1453) as the starting-point of the modern period,[1] perhaps because it was then that the axis of development shifted decisively from the Greek East to the European West.

The so-called "Renaissance" and the Protestant "Reformation" in central and western Europe were more or less still enclosed within a medieval outlook, and may be regarded more like "mere displacements, within the system of medieval Christendom."[2]

Certainly the term "modern" signals an antithesis to a specified past. In the last three centuries of European history the term expresses the affirmation of each successive *present*, of the up-to-date as fact and as point of departure for *progress*.

This is more than a proposition; it has become a habit of mind, an all-embracing mental outlook and way of life. Modern people doubt the absolute worth of what has been handed down, all established criteria or any validation derived from antiquity. This denial is not passive. It identifies itself with the dynamic of progress; it sets goals for evolutionary change; it constitutes a new perspective of human life.

The modern age signifies a break in all its aspects. Doubtless the matrix of the modern breaks with what was formerly permanent, self-evident and authoritative. The break itself defines the object of the search as a springboard for progress.

The modern age seeks the new, the unforeseen, the creative surprise. It is marked by the discovery of the New World, by revolutionary changes in scientific method, new technology, new ideas, new institutions, novel social and political forms. Radical discontinuities lurk behind the phenomenology of the new. It insists on breaking free from previous authority, all past cognitive criteria and regulative principles. The European medieval past was a religious past. Religion had priority in the life of the individual and of society. The Western Christian Church had been turned into a religious institution, controlling the educational system, scientific research, political functions and social outlook through its strict organizational structures. Europe's rupture with its medieval past was more or less anti-religious, anti-clerical and often inimical to ontological or regulative metaphysical principles.

This break with established religious tradition and authority defines the aims of the modern age, which aspires to a new conception of human activity, the world and History,[3] drawn from direct and verifiable experience, and centered on humankind and its capabilities. One is to live freed from the transcendent, from the authority of its religious institutionalization, and from the intellectual structures of theological proof.

This new outlook takes conscious or unconscious control over everyday life, people obeying a more and more generalized consensus. The demand for progress, effectiveness and empirical common sense implies a self-evident social program, and is resistant to any polemics that might challenge it. Presented in the seemly mantle of progress, the rupture with the past becomes self-explanatory and universally acceptable and shapes a new cosmogenetic culture.

The modern age is the most radically innovative culture in

history. Everything changes radically: our image of the world constructed by modern science, our social world, our manner of being. A new world picture is brought into existence, a new perception of reality, a new extended knowledge.

Old words now have new references. Terms for objects of knowledge or certain human activities have acquired an expanded or new meaning, pointing to new realities unacknowledged by people before. The word "electricity," for example, did not mean the same to Benjamin Franklin as it does to us today. The same is true for such words as "matter," "energy," "radiation;" or "information," "communications," "recreation," "dwelling," "agriculture;" or even "productivity," "consumption," "medical care," "household appliances," and a host of others.

The expansion of knowledge in the modern age makes one's head spin – whatever the original intentions, it leads to technology designed to make human life easier. These many and varied applications are identified with modern "development," which tends to foreground its own invincible dynamic of social acceptance. The modern European development goal pervades the universal and primary ideal of life, especially in countries which have not yet achieved it. Doubts and reservations about development as an ultimate goal usually refer to its exaggerated and absolutized logic in societies which already enjoy its benefits. Where development has not yet been achieved, fear of exaggeration and absolutization inhibits its pursuit.

The modern age is about the quest for development. New understanding of human existence and human action tend that way. Development gives modern life its meaning. It seems so primal, self-evident and imperative that other regulative principles or humanistic ideals take second place – even the refusal that one group of human beings exploit another. As Joan Robinson observes of some "Third World" countries: "the misery of being exploited by capitalists is nothing compared to the misery of not being exploited at all."[4]

2. Functionalism replaces the ontological approach

The modern understanding of being implies the deliberate abandonment of the ontological approach to the nature of reality.

Humanity in the modern age aims to explore every facet of reality and existence, everything that exists and happens. The furthest limits of microcosm and macrocosm must be accessible to the human mind. But reality interests us as objective phenomena and as functional constituents, not as existential fact. The very onticity of things ("being *qua* being"), or existence as the primary fact of our being, what we call the ontological problem, is marginal. Questions concerning the cause, end or purpose of existence, the causal principle or origin of beings, the relationships between things of the same kind, or between universal concepts and individual entities, no longer engage modern people.

This rejection is quite easily explained. Ontology is associated with intellectual arrogance and dogmatic inflexibility grounded in medieval thought. The dominant religious ideology of the European Middle Ages was based on the absolute priority of ontology. Obligatory apodictic, abstract interpretations of the facts of existence, limited research about what was knowable. Replacing empirical knowledge by abstract reasoning inspired an emphasis on ontology interpreted as the axiomatic superiority of the transcendent over the temporal and sensible, and as the absolute authority of that transcendent power's earthly representatives.

The breach with the medieval past presupposes breaking free from the ontological problem. Humanity in the modern age refuses to reconsider questions which trapped it for centuries in humiliating subservience to a hermeneutic and regulative straitjacket of axiomatic prohibitions. The modern rejection and marginalization of ontology is identified with empirical common sense, freedom of thought and research, and the pursuit of mathematical proof and experimental validation.

There seems no point in interpreting the fact of existence, or connecting it with some hypothetical and extra-empirical cause. Real things are of interest as part of "nature:" mathematics and experiment decode the rational assembly and function of the natural whole, making ontological interpretation superfluous. The human mind can make sense of real facts as firm or mutable functions and can intervene for utilitarian ends.

Humanity's claim to the greatest possible sovereignty over nature through the intellect highlights the functional understanding of nature as "becoming." Scientific observation tends to confirm nature's stable and immutable laws. It seeks in nature a strict conformity to laws, which implies determinism. Descartes, the English empiricists, French rationalists and Newton constructed a mechanistic image of the universe and its operation. The cosmos is a well-wound watch, and it is of minimal interest whether or not some God created it and set it in operation, since it now functions on its own with strict logical consistency. If we correctly decode how nature works, we can tame it to serve our own needs and goals.

This mechanistic image of the world extends into biology with La Mettrie's instructive but exaggerated book, *L'homme machine*, reaching a brilliant conclusion in Darwin's all-embracing theory of the evolution of species. Mechanistic interpretation is a methodological "constant" and guarantee of scientific validity, adopted as self-evidently true by the social sciences. The "scientific" character of social science presupposes classifying life phenomena under measurable constants which permit inference. Observation defines consistently repeated behavioral phenomena under the same conditions, so causal laws can be formulated. Interdependent causes and effects in collective behavior may be articulated as a rational system. Positive *prediction* then becomes a utilitarian justification of scientific systematization.

A scientific approach to society means sidestepping ontological questions – human beings are assimilated to "physical atoms," as neutral units of the social whole. If Darwinian anthropology becomes the self-evident basis of the social sciences, the existential enigma of subjective otherness can be set aside. A human being is a biological unity taking its place with every other link in the chain of development from simpler and less perfect to more complex and complete organisms, a development governed by the implacable law of "natural selection."[5] The instinct of self-preservation forms and controls social symbiosis, which is a product of the power of this impulse to make choices.

In this way justice and morality are detached from any metaphysical claim. The concept of the "natural individual" inspires the logic of "natural justice," and the rationalistic regulative principles of ethics have become "autonomous," as in the utilitarian "social contract."

The art of politics is likewise organized as a methodical "science" balancing the social individual's rights and obligations. This is the age of the "rights of the individual." The idea of equal rights is derived from the generally accepted natural likeness of individuals and their basic biological similarity. The balancing of rights and obligations replaces interest in the ontological problem, questions posed by the free play of social forces, and the undetermined aspects of interpersonal relations.

Parallel to this, political science interprets and programs human problems about production and exchange, as if the natural individual were a unit of production and consumption. Units are assimilated to each other by reducing them to the lowest common denominator, that every person produces and consumes goods and services. The variety of human production is reduced to a view of "labor" as "productive power," identified with utilitarian means of production. At the same time, the depersonalized "human unit" is judged according to byproducts of the economic "mechanism" such as: "per capita income," "per capita product," "mean purchasing power," "man-hours" for the measurement of productivity, etc. – or else it functions as a constant for constructing abstract macro-economic concepts, such as the work force, the gross national product, the average yield, the mean purchasing power, etc.

This mechanistic cosmology and analogous anthropology of social and practical priorities assume the axiological "progress" of humanity and nature. The demand for progress breaks with medieval ontology. In practice it avoids stressing metaphysics or transcendence, even sacrificing the very progress that is being pursued. But the axiological progress of humanity and nature is less worrying than the brutal change in their ontological interpretation.

Pseudo-science and assertions about meaning pervade the modern age, devaluing if not cheapening both humankind and nature without any protest. The theory of evolution has been popularized as a simple descent of humankind from the apes,[6] and people want to believe that life and intelligent beings exist on other planets in spite of scientific research to the contrary.[7] Modern humanity seems unable to endure ontological superiority and existential uniqueness. We insist on cheapening ourselves, on submitting ourselves to natural dependence and needs, claiming for ourselves the existential level of an animal and the randomness of nature. This rationalistic "realism" seeking a "hold on an inferred reality" and a "deliverance from every metaphysical illusion," is probably itself another delusion.

3. Utilitarian rationalism

Throughout the European Middle Ages, intellectualism aspired to metaphysical support and transcendent validity: Individual human understanding was dependent on humanity's creation "in the image of God," constituting a miniature version of divine understanding. Correct use of the mind ("rational thought" or "thinking rationally") implied an ability to approach the "essential" knowledge of reality. The correct use of these mental capabilities was inferred as a formal method derived from the mind's own demand for certainty, and its mode of operation was taken to be innate. The European Middle Ages acknowledged Aristotle as the philosopher who best transformed the demand for intellectual certainty into a formal method.

First the modern age refutes the metaphysical defense of intellectualism, then attempts to deny it more radically, inevitably referring to the natural individual's "spirituality." It attempts to rely on empiricism and sense-perceptions, but empiricism subsequently creates problems which clearly impede scientific progress: Sense data prove less reliable than mathematical logic, preventing the formation of comprehensive (mainly cosmological) theories.

Thinkers of the Enlightenment, the forerunners of the modern age, had to return to intellectualism in a naturalistic interpretation. They considered intellection as a purely biological cerebral function – "it is matter itself which under certain conditions produces spirit." Moreover, intellection was humanity's naturally given way to grasp the articulation, structure and function of objective reality. There was a given correlation between human "reason" and the "law" of nature, linking individual mental processes and the construction of the natural whole.

Finally, Kant's impressive "critical" postulate reconciled intellectualism and empiricism and imposed a generally approved empirically justified intellectualism and an intellectually sustained empiricism on the modern age. Our understanding judges the epistemological data of sensory experience, individual understanding replacing the transcendentally given "*logos*." The *critical* function of the mind moves from the sensory perception of phenomena to their comprehension and then constructs the concept – unifying phenomena of the same kind into a concept.

The gulf between absolute subjectivity and comparable absolute objectivity remains unbridgeable. Modern humanity is preoccupied with this problem, searching for objective primary factors to constitute the epistemological functioning of the subject, and their equivalent for objective criteria to validate the knowledge which has been attained; no other metaphysic is of interest. Anything "meta" or "beyond" physical reality is merely the problem of our epistemological approach to it, and of the objective validity of the method we choose.

A striking characteristic of the modern age is how it transcends even the epistemological contradictions or problems in the utilitarian evaluation of knowledge. Utilitarian evaluation focuses on the priority (axiological, functional) of the intellective or empirical approach to knowledge, and also on the universality of criteria for the objective validity of knowledge. In such an epistemology the emphasis is on the relationship between signifier and signified, not primarily as a "real" (valid) correspondence between the intellective and the sensible, or as a definitive way of using the signifier, but on their relationship as a convention for the utilitarian exploitation of what is signified. The shift from meaning to use was made by Wittgenstein on the basis of the function of language: "What signs fail to express, their application shows. What signs slur over, their application says clearly."[8]

The utilitarian functionality of knowledge, going beyond any conventional character of the linguistic code, attains a "validity of communication" for both science and (chiefly) social practice. Knowledge comes to be accepted functionally by referring to specific indicators of effectiveness and benefit even if it is potentially deceptive. "Validity of communication" presupposes "consent" based precisely on the priority of a measurable beneficial result. The causal interdependence presupposed by validity of communication, consent and affirmation could define utilitarian rationalism as perhaps the most representative characteristic of the modern age.

Even medieval intellectualism tended towards utilitarian effectiveness, mainly by imposing the prevailing ideology by incontrovertible proof. The medieval period benefited from the effective use of a metaphysically valid rationalism. But modern utilitarian rationalism reverses the terms of verification: correct thought arises from measurable effectiveness. Rationalism is valid so far as it is utilitarian, or functionally productive.

By following circumstantial and contingent criteria and thus repudiating ontology or consciously avoiding it, we do not resolve the problem of the recognition of general regulative principles. The standard applied may be derived from "development," and the progress of science and technology. Social ideologies and aims of "general happiness" may offer ideological criteria which are often legitimized by self-deception about individuals' imaginary relationships with the real conditions of their existence.[9] Collective myths of racial superiority, or the messianic mission of some social order may suggest evaluative criteria.

This lack of valid criteria prevents rationalistic effectiveness from being discussed and evaluated. Coherent values are abandoned in favor of mere rhetoric referring only to the utilitarian result of the rationalistic process, which appears self-evidently and universally approved. Utilitarian rationalism is validated by its functional productivity, regardless of how it is evaluated. Procedural or practical rationality, often accompanied by blasts of anathema, is part of the "physiognomy" of the modern age: including the methodical industrialized murder in the Nazi camps and the Gulag psychiatric institutions.

To abandon claims to universal axioms inevitably relativizes the persuasive power of rationalism, presupposing that mere "consent," significance or "meaning" is limited to the affirmation of use. The affirmation of specific utilitarian results defines the communicative logic of particular social groups, political parties or professional bodies – collective consents and resistance pivot around them. A choice of values, priorities and criteria is created (a "pluralism of points of view"), but they all depend on the utilitarian verification of rationalism.

4. Regulative eudaemonism

Modern society is "pluralistic," especially for regulative principles of human conduct. It is often characterized as a "tolerant" society, "tolerating" and legitimizing different preferences, priorities and criteria.

Different value systems and the tolerance of difference function with utilitarian rationalism as their common basis. Even after upheavals in modern epistemology, the relativization of and radical doubts about the rationalistic method, the collapse of mechanistic determinism, and the demonstration that "signifiers" are mere conventions even in mathematical proof, utilitarian rationalism shapes the practical side of life and the mental makeup of modern society.

To affirm utilitarian rationalism independently of scientific/cognitive validation reflects the primary social need for regulative principles. The regulative principles articulate certain social needs, ordering them on a scale of priorities. The values expressed in the regulative principles are not there by chance but represent specific needs – the product of real needs. Ordering needs on a scale of values by differentiating between priorities molds the different cultural forms or "levels."

In the European Middle Ages, humanity's religious needs manifestly took priority. Whether they were generated spontaneously, or whether the dominant ideology imposed them on Western society is of secondary significance. Regulative principles came into force and became accepted, because not only religious sentiments but real needs of a religious character were given priority in every aspect of medieval life.

The hierarchy of our common needs helps establish the modern "paradigm." The "salvation of the soul," a life of beatitude beyond death, ceases to be modern humanity's chief need. We come to prefer the affirmation of earthly life, the celebration of matter and the body, the strengthening of the individual, the recognition of the equality of the natural rights between people, the opportunity for all to advance towards a life of ease and material prosperity, the subjection of nature to productivity as a benefit to humanity.

Religious needs are not extinguished in the modern age. Certainly they are limited and repudiated. But chiefly they are ordered differently. A pleasant life on earth takes precedence, and religion follows this primary need and serves it. That religion concerns itself with practical-moral benefits, such as utilitarian good works, protecting public morals, or providing psychological support for individuals, or acquiring social power. In the modern age, there is a consumer relationship between the individual and religion, as with art and education. The individual consumes religious assurance or enjoyment, just as he or she consumes artistic pleasure, education and cultural "products."[10] The need to consume comes first, and this shapes other criteria and practices.

Needs and their ordering in a hierarchy come first, and the framing of regulative principles follows. So the "pluralism" of regulative principles in the modern age is nothing new. Placing needs in a hierarchy must fragment and differentiate indispensable regulative principles.

The multiform hierarchy of needs with its concomitant "pluralism" evidently has its "own interior logic" which is consciously or unconsciously *eudaemonistic*. The logic of eudaemonism presupposes the tolerance and affirmation of multiple preferences, freedom of choice, and differentiation between goals for intended benefits. Only individual and collective eudaemonism can be tolerated, permitting or producing a multiform hierarchy of needs and the concomitant pluralism of regulative principles.

Broadening the principles of "democracy" into multiform legitimization of utilitarian behavior is typical of regulative eudaemonism in the modern age.

The principles, origins and roots of parliamentary "democracy" betray an "internal logic" that is manifestly eudaemonistic. This logic excludes any ontological conception of politics, any pursuit of existential authenticity: the ancient Greek postulate that political "truth" is to be identified with "society"[11] and the Christian ideal of the communion of persons, "imaging" the Triadic Archetype of true life,[12] are both absent. The aim of modern "democracy" is the utilitarian strengthening of individuals' rights, assuring their quality of life and protecting their freedom of choice.

Such eudaemonism is translated into regulative principles that balance rights and obligations, so that the rights of each person in a democracy are limited by the respect due to the rights of others. These values of respect for one's own rights and the rights of other individuals or social groups vary in relation to one's personal or collective hierarchy of needs. Different hierarchies of the fundamental needs of life exist – what each person regards as primary or secondary needs – so do needs for social security, employment, material comfort, housing, information, recreation. These different hierarchies are translated into a multiform limitation of reciprocal rights and a "pluralism" of regulative principles; the limitations on rights are valued and compared in very different ways according to the effort involved in the work, the importance of the task, the contribution to society, the need for consumption, the capacity to contribute taxes, and equality of opportunity.

Values are judged according to the common eudaemonistic logic of democracy. These judgments need utilitarian legitimacy within the framework of the "pluralism" of "democratic" functions. The trade union movement that puts pressure on the employer is the employee's "democratic right," but anti-strike action and the protection of his property is a "democratic right" of the employer. The citizen has access to information as a "democratic right," but the media have a right to profit from their businesses. Hence information obeys the rules of the marketplace. Voters choose their political party as a "democratic right," but the parties also have a "democratic right" to attract votes with psychological marketing strategies. In a modern democracy universal principles of political conduct cannot exist, only a systematic balancing of the demands created and legitimized by regulative eudaemonism.

One could find comparable examples of regulative eudaemonism from almost any area of modern social life: from the economy,[13] the trade union movement, the philosophy of education and the organization of the educational system, the logic of the problematics and discussions of "bioethics," etc.

Perhaps the most characteristic examples of the influence of regulative eudaemonism on our social mentality may be seen in generalized changes in very ancient customs concerning love and death. The institution of marriage, whose origins are lost in the depths of prehistory, and also grief for a deceased member of the family, are perceptibly transformed for the first time. The changes consistently follow the presuppositions of eudaemonistic logic and are expressed in universal regulative principles: tolerance and approval of alternative sexual preferences, organized demands for the legal "right" to be different, the manipulation of instinctual needs by marketing, the commercial organization of entertainment and fashion. Death is systematically excluded from the family home, burial procedures are industrialized, the symbols of grief are limited and soon removed, hospitals and insurance companies deal with death according to economics and the logic of statistics.

Eudaemonism has clearly usurped the place of ontology in the modern age: it is, rather, the dominant response to the conscious or unacknowledged question concerning the *meaning* of human existence and human activity. The initial eudaemonistic conception indisputably functions as the matrix of regulative principles.

5. Ideologies of hope

Part of the characteristic "physiognomy" of the modern age is the transposition of social perspectives into ideological blueprints and teleologies.

The term "ideology" owes its origin to the first theoretical schematizations of the modern age: Destutt de Tracy first used it in 1796, marking the start of the faith of the Enlightenment that social reform would result from the reorganization of ideas:[14] Only when people's ideas change – their individual perceptions, convictions and interpretation of reality, their understanding of nature and history, of goals and obligations, of the meaning of existence and of life – do new and desired social forms emerge.

The demand for new "ideas" implies that the change must be expressed as a system and put into effect. If "ideas" need to be changed, the existing ones must be mistaken and harmful. Confirmed error or harmfulness justifies putting forward a counter-proposal, legitimizing the effort of imposition.

Thus ideology is engendered by the logic of breaking with, and struggling against, the past. It becomes specific, proposing new ideas which people must embrace if they are to liberate themselves as individuals and as a society from the "darkness" of the medieval past: ideas which block progress towards the forms of society to which they aspire are to be set aside and faith in the desired goals is to be imposed on all.

Such demands ignore marginal areas where new ideas can be engendered naturally from the needs of the social body. The ideology dominates because its adherents are convinced that prevailing ideas are wrong and harmful. The correct and more profitable ideas are framed in advance without reference to the social body. The ideology interprets social and individual needs, the needs which people *ought* to have, by itself and *a priori*. And it systematically imposes previously framed ideas.

Ideology is by definition a rationalist construct. It emerges from the rational criticism of existing ideas, and its own counter-proposal cannot but be based on rational arguments, on "objectively" valid blueprints of the intended social perspective. Rationalistic systematization over-anticipates social needs, and would have had no chance of success without the goal of arousing collective desires at the same time. Collective and general desires spring from innate drives, such as the self-preservation urge or the egocentric quest for power.

Accordingly, ideology represents something more than its proposed new perceptions, convictions and interpretations. It can transform desire into a conviction-interpretation-goal, which does not need to correspond to the actual circumstances of life, seeing that these are to be transformed. Starting from rational motives for changing reality, ideology often transforms its own rationalism into mysticism, achieving a complete denial of reality for the sake of the desired illusion. Freud demonstrated how this "power of illusion" functions, and later studies have based an impressive critique of modern ideology on Freud.[16]

Certainly, the function of ideologies in the modern age is complicated, contributing to the "physiognomy" of modern societies; ideologies have replaced the ontology that has been rejected or consciously marked as spurious. The "soteriological" character of ideologies, means they promise to fulfil collective hopes.

Ideologies do not respond directly to ontological questions – nor do they aspire to do so. They are always clearly anthropocentric and sociocentric: they promise institutional and organizational change in society as a whole, in labor relations and in the functioning of the economy, which will lead to "general happiness." Ideology weaves together schematic programs with eudaemonistic promises, thereby mating rationalism with incompatible cherished illusions.

This shotgun marriage always has its invisible or unacknowledged ontological presuppositions, which help ideology establish its self-evident, if not obligatory, acceptance. Modern social ideologies typically ignore questions concerning the causal principle of existence, subjective self-awareness, the modal absoluteness of existential otherness, the definitive relativity of the subject, or any other mostly unanswered question. Social ideologies work on the level of collective desires and eudaemonistic promises with concomitant anthropocentric criteria presupposing the "random" principle of existence, and a correlative agnosticism. They conceive of existence, nature and history on the assumption of the existential fact's axiomatic self-sufficiency, a human autonomy unfettered by ideas about causality or providence.

This existential autonomy explains the power of ideologies in the goal of "progress." Within this ideological framework, human beings aspire to be managers of their hopes, creators of their own future. Nature with its rich capabilities and energy sources is waiting for the human mind to tame it, intervening in its innermost functioning to satisfy the need for comfort and ease. Ideologies propose ways and means for a more productive management of humanity's existential autonomy, which can be imposed to constitute a hope of "progress" and "general happiness." The element of hope, the eudaemonistic promise – either material or spiritual – constitutes the ideological dynamic. The ideologies of hope, from realistic rationalist schemes to the wildest utopian illusions, have largely formed the modern age.

Prolegomena 2

The Collapse Of The Modern Vision

1. The end of logical positivism

Belief in the self-evident rationality of the positive knowledge derived from the "correct" logical method shapes the "physiognomy" of the modern age. The modern way of life is based on the belief that utilitarian rationalism works and on the practical consequences that flow from this.

The self-evident universality of common-sense rationality disdains metaphysics: it does not consider humanity to be created "in the image of God," and denies the medieval vision of the human intellect as a version of the mind of God. Modern rationality belongs to human nature and relates to the natural functioning of the human mind. Common-sense rationality remains universal – accessible to all: Rational conclusions and claims can sustain scientific validity and regulative principles for the common life.

The conclusions and claims are "rational" when sustained by clear thought and repeatable experiment. A clearly articulated methodology ensures clarity of thought and critical control which confirm the validity of the experiment. Methodical, critical and experimental proof guarantees common-sense validity, that is, correct rationality. Every person can recognize what is rational and what is not methodically, critically and experimentally, and accept it as a universal regulative principle.

This universal capability is easily transformed into a general and "objective" claim. Methodical rationality becomes a model decrying every form of relativism or skepticism which is part of the assimilation of approaches to knowledge to changing social practice. The otherness of rational and empirical relations with the real is undermined. The rational code receives a bogus authenticity.

The modern universal concept of *rights* has been founded on common-sense logic. We call a right the advantage derived from what is commonly recognized as just: it recognizes or guarantees claims and needs based on the universally accepted principles of a legal code. The universally adopted code for the modern age is natural reason, the "naturally just:" recognizing or guaranteeing rational claims and needs of ordinary human nature. As a natural individual every human being has rights in common with everyone else, needs and claims justified by the logic of nature. Human rights are derived only from the logic of natural needs or claims, not from racial descent, social origin and class, inherited property or anything else.

The right to satisfy natural needs and claims has an immediate common-sense universality. But nature differentiates between individual needs and the intensity of individual claims. Satisfying differentiated needs and claims rationally therefore requires systematic compensation for natural differences. A commonly accepted implementation of this in the modern age takes the specific form of the *social contract.* Institutional conventions with a strictly methodical rationality seek to balance individual rights and obligations, in the pursuit of a common harmonious symbiosis. The modern development of jurisprudence, the scientific study of law, results from laborious effort in every aspect of human relations – it has become indispensable because the regulative role of reason and the social contract need to be made explicit.

Translating the rational balancing of individual rights and obligations into the methodology of science changed the social contract itself into a general "objective" demand, and therefore an axiomatic imperative. Legal institutionalization of the social contract aims to unite individual assents, but the "objective" logic of institutionalization presupposes controlled assents. Institutional logic attacks not only inequalities but also qualitative differentiations, becoming part of the standardization of individual approaches to social reality. In the name of an impersonal "objective" logic, the "democratic" institutions of the social contract tend towards an authoritarian character: they impose or replace assent, instead of eliciting and coordinating it. In the "parliamentary democracies," social assent may be limited to a periodic general election. This is simply the rational legitimation of the transfer of authority to all-powerful "functionaries" of the state machine.

Universal belief in the validity of rationality was first challenged in the natural sciences. Experimental research and increasingly sophisticated instruments of observation gradually raised doubts about mechanistic rationality in natural processes. Confidence in common-sense logic, which sought to transcribe reality into defined, stable "signifiers" understood identically by every subjective mind, is no longer sustainable.

The meaning of natural law, natural "stability," the causal correlation of phenomena now owed more to the powers of scientific observation than to the nature of what was observed. The "tool-like" relativity of the rational method, the polymorphous character of verification rules, the replacement of common-sense representation by reductionist mathematical "languages" began to appear. The real difference between *signifiers* and things *signified* was confirmed: what was signified could not be reduced to the objectivity of the signifiers of conventional categories.

The next step was parallel to the developments in physical epistemology, raising doubts about dogmatic rationality in social practice. The rational method was taken for granted and its automatic effectiveness devalued and alienated the human subject. People began to notice the symptoms and denounced the rational modeling of society with its self-evident dogmatism obliterating subjective otherness. They protested at the denial of fundamental human needs for the sake of an autonomous rational process.

Rationalized production, making methods and goals autonomous, and planning the division of labor were early symptoms of reducing human beings to neutral appendages of mechanistic processes. The rational organization of consumption, the stimulation of consumer needs, autonomous market manipulation, advertising as "brainwashing" tend the same way.

In politics the axiomatic rationality of ideologies claims a self-evident validity, sabotaging and destroying social demands by imposing a logic of "general happiness." Certain social reforms, organized movements and revolutionary uprisings claimed to be "by the people" but were carried out "for the people" and in the name of the people by small tyrannical oligarchies.

In the rational exercise of power, productivity began to appear incompatible with democratic processes and institutions. In modern societies, power inescapably becomes technocratic and frees itself from social control; economic planning must obey market logic regardless of social needs and the national budget. "Democratic" government decisions which change people's lives are dictated by considerations freed from all legal control and are sometimes defended on the inviolable grounds of "national security."

The logic of "development" seems scarcely compatible with the logic of democracy and individual rights. The pursuit of material benefits favors "development." The need for investment often requires the state to reduce labor costs and devalue workers' income, sometimes also introducing authoritarian anti-strike laws, anti-democratic restrictions and control of trade unions. The logic of development sometimes leads to large-scale dismissals of workers, since unemployment is the price for controlling inflation, causing social hardship and the psychological and moral humiliation of the unemployed.

The labor movement inevitably resists the anti-democratic logic of development, resorting to similarly anti-democratic retaliation by strikes with their "social cost." The logic is the same: all contributors to "development" demanding a practical participation in the benefits of "the good life" that "development" procures.

Making the economy independent of social needs also releases politics from serving social needs. Politics becomes a professional career demanding ever greater disposable economic capital to compete in the "marketplace" of popular preferences. Pre-election programs call for vast expenditure, as part of the rationalistic marketplace. Political ideologies and promises influence voters with the commercial logic of supply and demand. Demand is systematically organized to stimulate consumer interest: political promises are presented as merchandise which must have attractive packaging. Party political programs are transformed into seductive slogans by advertising specialists skilled in the "science" of marketing.

Rationalistic efficiency has transformed modern politics into a systematized psychological war of images. Everyone appeals to democratic institutions, although subordinating them to party priorities in practice.

The press and television inevitably take the lead. The commercial development of printed and electronic information makes it less informative: information and analysis are subordinated to sensationalism, circulation figures or ratings, and the compromises of marketplace politics. Facts are obliterated by interpretations of facts, "pluralism" means versions arranged for vested interests. The media rarely address the citizen's reason and judgment. They target sentiment, hidden impulses, and the faceless subject's need to access identity from ideologies or political parties.

Positivist rationalism is relentless, goals are selected unthinkingly; this is often denounced as the dead end for modernity.[1] The Enlightenment's early faith in common-sense logic, and the power of correct reasoning over everybody, is catastrophically utopian, since it has been broken up into as many unshakeable "logics" as there are interest groups or even individual aspirations.

In referring to the collapse of belief in an "objective" rationality, I do not imply that human reason or its effective functioning is worthless. The rational method has grown free of the functioning of society; rationalism becomes an instrument of antisocial, egocentric autarky. Rather than being judged by its capacity to facilitate participation in the human experience, it is judged by aptness for positive work defined by the method itself; and by the power of the method to impose itself and produce results. Human symbiosis in the modern age creates communities of uncommunicating individuals, condemned to hesitate between obedience and rebellion, because interpersonal communion has declined. The security of private individuals has become an obsession and the "city," founded on egocentric self-preservation, is culturally impoverished.

2. Antisocial subjectivity

At the beginning of the modern age, individualism inspired polemics. It openly confronted the medieval preference for the general and the universal with institutions, structures and principles which aimed to make individuals uniformly submissive and equal. The theoretical efforts to define "substance" and formulate the "goal" led to totalitarian collective practices which endowed the individual with value on the authority of metaphysics. They imposed similar kinds of behavior and perceptions, limiting or excluding active affirmation of subjective otherness.

Even the medieval religious outlook in the West was individualistic. It aimed at individual salvation through practices designed to reassure the individual by dwelling on individual guilt, individual redemption from guilt, and individual justification by redemption. Roman Catholic dogmatic intellectualism and legalistic morality are founded on self-evident individual self-sufficiency (of intellect and will), on the claim to an individualistic autarky. They excluded the social realization of personal otherness through the communion of relations.

At the same time, however, intellectualism and moralism insisted on the importance of "objectivism," the catholic and the general, which consoles and protects the individual. Methods, principles and codes which guarantee "objectivity" convey reassuring certainties to the individual, while taking absolute control over them, adapting and subjecting them to the universal power. Every social totalitarianism (religious, political or any other) manifests this phenomenological negation, which is very effective: it is grounded, consciously or unconsciously, on the desire for individualistic (chiefly psychological) assurance, which is dressed up in aspirations to "objective" goals and the embrace of generalized certainties. The initial priority of the individual over the communal is easily abandoned for the leveling submission to institutionalized "objectives." Arguments for individualism in the modern age failed to diagnose this tragic dialectic and therefore took it for granted. The Enlightenment broke with institutionalized medieval "objectivities," substituting others stripped of any *a priori* metaphysical validity.

Modernist culture highlighted individuals, their rights and liberties, their valuation of themselves, the infinite choices offered by political and economic liberalism. But individualistic desires and demands had to be derived from "objectivities" functioning as regulative principles in order to be imposed socially. The methodology was simple: tracing the individual back to the general, subjective choice back to universal obligation. Common "nature" secured its positivistic validity: an "objective" rationality could be based on every individual's natural rationality, his or her innate moral will implying an impartial volitional "ought." The individual mind's representational capability could correspond to the "rationality" of the cosmic whole.

Tracing the individual back to the general, or subjective demand back to universal obligation, leads to a neutralized and standardized version of the individual. Whenever individual need clashes with "objective" obligation, there is no good reason for the priority of the "objective." The "objective" results from making the individual absolute and autonomous, so no longer means anything. If "objectivity" is to function as a regulative principle, it too must be freed from the necessity which produced it and be imposed on individuals. State structures, rationalistic legislation, regulative ideologies, party political and trade union institutions have become autonomous, and take responsibility for imposing it.

The constant production of goods as a prerequisite of "development" and "progress" is an authoritarian compulsion. "Development" and "progress" are measurable in a national economy, and objectify the individual demand for the good life. But the economy functions by something other than individual demands, obeying the need to impose constant production on individuals, not by choice but as an obligation.

The obligation is often invisible, but society as a whole insists on the constant widening of consumer choices, which is clearly artificial and directed by advertising. This second imperative makes the obligation to produce more acceptable.

Thus production and consumption operate independently of the real needs of individuals. They impose exclusively quantitative priorities on human life, turning subjective otherness into undifferentiated individualism. Individuals become passive units of production and consumption, while alienation is squeezed from them as if it were true enjoyment.

The advancement of individualism, a characteristic element of modernity, functions as the inexorable alienation of humanity. It has nothing to do with the "alienation" of the proletarian masses prophesied by Karl Marx. Modernity's alienation is discreet and imperceptible, but above all eudaemonistic. Its leveling but hedonistic individualism unceasingly refutes subjectivity.

What is this form of individualism which refutes subjectivity? Think of people with socially assimilated behavior and mentality, who proclaim their egocentric individualism but whose behavior and mentality conform to an imposed code. They allow no margin for subjective otherness. Their conformity with the dominant model does not imply common goals and aspirations. Their goals and aspirations remain irremediably egotistical, concentrating on individual interests. Individual or collective means, not ends, mold outlook and behavior.

Concentration on egocentric aspirations expresses mostly quantitative preferences; otherness of subjects and outlooks demands a qualitative unique content. All communication is useless, as only otherness is shared, while the quantitative pursuit of goods is imposed or fudged. Communication is replaced by measuring quantitative preferences. Dialogue uses the stiff "wooden" language of established convention.

Much activity in the modern age lacks imagination, originality and creative inspiration. Social processes like collective demands, systematic treatments, successive proposals, renovating initiatives appear aimed at the same individualistic goals, constructed on utilitarian grounds. Modern "pluralism" becomes parallel and divergent monologues, replacing the dynamic of dialogue. The lack of communion destroys every possibility of agreement.

The words "dialogue" and "assent" now express a one-sided pluralism: the demand for individualistic aspirations to be mutually compatible and tolerate each other. And when the mutual compatibility weakens the effectiveness of the aspirations, then "dialogue" and "assent" consist of that institutionalizing or organizing power of aggressive rival aspirations finally imposed by whoever disposes of the strongest power of coercion.

Individualism makes modern individuals assimilate to each other and become uniform, which destroys subjective otherness. The basis of social relations is undermined. The measuring of status and mutual rivalry become more important. Individualistic demands exclude the ethics of dialogue, and the struggle for self-transcendence, forming communities of uncommunicating individuals.

Inescapably, the innate human need for sociability seeks imaginary social fulfillment. Power struggles aspire to the dignity of politics and function as illusory conflicts between social programs and ideologies. Programs and proposals have little relevance to social needs, for the most part camouflaging the pursuit of power by individuals or interest groups.

Psychological recourse to organized political groups ensures a certain identity for individuals deprived of every subjective distinguishing mark. The invocation of "nature" and the rights of the individual provide useful guarantees but not an identity of existential uniqueness and difference. The modern age is aggressively secular, depriving individuals of the innermost knowledge of subjectivity and identity that comes with reference to a creator God who exercises providential care over his creation.

Any organized political party, ideology or "leader" or "generalissimo" can function as a substitute for this existential subjectivity. In this sense politics in the modern age is in some respects a "transformation of the religious urge."[2] There is no need to add examples of ideologies turning into religious faith, dressing up leaders in myth and worship. They are almost commonplace. And this concerns not merely the eclipse of the sacred but the substitution of politics for existence. "The political becomes existential (place of the existent); it is identified with Being."[3] In certain circumstances, love, art and the understanding of death are subordinated to political fantasizing: the leader and/or the party become pure objects of erotic devotion, art submits to ideological "realism," death is regarded as a political act or challenge in mass conflicts.

The substitution of politics for existence is the supreme betrayal of the subjective otherness of man. When humanity's being is wholly contained within the political process, it is condemned to programmed behavior, a uniform outlook, a predetermined psychology. Marcuse's "One-dimensional Man"[4] reveals precisely the kind of alienation which objective conditions impose on human life, also adopted by individuals committed to political totalitarianism.

Beyond hyper-production, hyper-consumption, the organized pursuit of individual rights and politicization, technological developments also nurture antisocial subjectivity, although they should make human life easier. The widening access to domestic technology is probably the most important.

In "advanced" modern societies, a child grows up knowing the most vital aspects of reality are subject to its individual will: the touch of a switch brings access to light or heating or music or television. By turning a tap it has hot or cold water, and its food is prepackaged for minimum preparation. Clothing in its exact size is available ready-made in the shops. The telephone assures communication with every corner of the world. Distances shrink with the development of transport or are annihilated by television.

In earlier forms of social life, the satisfaction of basic human needs required an effort, an overcoming of the resistance of nature. To overcome resistance, human beings struggled with nature from their first steps in life, engaging in constant empirical study, immediate contact, communion and dialogue with intractable nature. Lighting the fire, drawing water, cultivating the land to provide food, producing clothes, made human beings participators and sharers in natural reality. They were subject to its rules and assumptions, not self-evident masters and sovereigns over it.

In modern societies more and more people make nothing and devote themselves to non-material undertakings as employees, freelance professionals, businessmen, entrepreneurs. Mere consumption nurtures involuntary and unconscious subjectivity which takes mastery and sovereignty over nature for granted. The vast technology to satisfy human needs destroys all propensity towards ascetic limitation of desire, or engaging in "dialogue" with resisting forces. Apart from economic limitations, only legal prohibitions limit desire: statutes designed to make one conform to whatever prevails in society or is imposed by the state. Legal restrictions unavoidably beg the question: who imposed them, why and with what authority?

Education, art, love, are tainted by egocentric consumerism, its conventions and fads. In the school classroom, university auditorium or concert hall, the layout and seating arrangement symbolize or presuppose individualized giving and consumerist receiving, hindering inter-subject communion. Knowledge is offered ready for consumption by guaranteed providers and tailored to individual receptivity, entertainment is consumed individually and is purchased at a price proportionate to the skill of the performers. Knowledge and art do not constitute a social event, people are not invited to join in, personal experience is not solicited.[5]

Loveless people are incapable of transcending themselves, or sharing their wishes and desires, or entering into dialogue, or joining in a journey, or participating in life and experience.

That the words "eros" and "erotic" refer to sex (and often to pornography alone) is characteristic of the modern age. Erotic attraction is openly commercialized, supports the sex industry, and is universally used as an advertising technique to arouse consumer interest in any product whatsoever.

Art, better than any sociology, echoes the emptiness and loneliness of non-social existence, of antisocial subjectivity. The founding basis of liberated humanity in the modern age is individualism which seems to trap us in tormenting alienation from true subjectivity.

3. The non-coincidence of communication and language

The use of language, its syntactic structure and its objective meaning, have been modernity's last resort in defining criteria of logical validity. After orthodox rationalism was radically undermined, and faith in the regulative rationality of "natural justice" or the "social contract" collapsed, hope of framing a valid utilitarianism was transposed to the "naturally" given communicative power of language.

The genius of Wittgenstein showed the supreme importance of language as a regulative constant in scientific formulation. He demonstrated with clarity that the logic of language is representative of the logic of the cosmos, reflecting the pictorial logic of facts as they are, and thus "it is laid against reality like a measure."[6] We cannot separate the logic of language from its signifying-imaging function. Language is an image of reality. It shows the logical form of reality – it presents it. If we recognize the logical syntax of any kind of linguistic semantic, all logical propositions, and the whole of physical science are already given.

Wittgenstein's analysis may have been productive but it did not satisfy modernity's demand for a "linguistic positivism." The correspondence between linguistic logic and the logic of physical reality has been regarded as a transcendental- metaphysical given, and consequently a dogmatic *a priori* which did not accord with the demands of "scientific" positivism. Wittgenstein himself declared unequivocally that "logic is transcendental;"[7] and therefore "propositions can represent the whole of reality, but they cannot represent what they must have in common with reality in order to be able to represent it – logical form."[8] Precisely because its function is only representational, language cannot articulate the meaning of the cosmos either. It cannot express in words either its ethics or its aesthetics.[9] Therefore linguistic positivism cannot provide regulative objectivity and is useless for the social sciences. Philosophy itself, by ignoring the function of language to make an image of reality, is dominated by confusion and incomprehension. The work of philosophy can be nothing other than "critique of language," that is, the clarification of the boundaries of natural science.[10]

The search for a "linguistic positivism" which would validate utilitarianism in scientific discourse persists in Otto Neurath and Rudolf Carnap's attempt to locate truth not in the representational function of language but in language itself – the meaning of words and the logical syntax of sentences. They sought an immediate logical clarity in fundamental propositions (protocol statements) which do not need verification, because they function with a self-evident accessible meaning and syntactic validity. Thus any system of scientific propositions can be verified as a combination of several commonly received simple propositions.

Apart from the epistemological questions left unanswered by this project, Quine attacked it as another form of dogmatism, since it presupposed *a priori* the existence of truth within the logical syntax of the proposition and in the meaningful sequence of the words. Quine proved indisputably that the concept of truth must be regarded as unfounded within consistent positivism.

Next Alfred Tarski tried to salvage the concept of truth, stripped of every ontological content or reference to reality:

Within the given language "in use" (which he called "meta-language") we can fashion partial languages (which he called "formalized") for every branch of science, with precise blue-prints of the logical structure of propositions and the burden of meaning of words, which do not signify reality but the particular way in which reality is used in every branch of science. The verification of the significance of concepts in formalized language refers only to the manner of use-understanding of the particular concepts in the metalanguage, and consequently the "truth" of the linguistic propositions remains functionally positivistic.

Tarski's proposal simply intensified the crisis of "linguistic positivism," since it relied on a "validity" unrelated to scientific propositions or an objective world, linguistic terms or meanings and objective reference. Later epistemologists who studied this problem tended to abandon the need for a fixed methodological "objectivity" or diachronic validity.

Karl Popper introduced the "principle of falsification" of scientific propositions. They are always provisional and are used in expectation of their eventual refutation and replacement by new propositions which will account for a greater number of phenomena or will extend the possibilities of controlling them in a subjective and empirical manner. Thomas Kuhn then suggested that the validity of scientific theories and formulations should be accepted only within the context of a universal "paradigm," within the totality of conceptual, experimental and methodological assumptions which characterize a period or a "scientific community."

Hilary Putnam in consequence insisted on transposing epistemological verification from the requirement for unassailable correctness to how scientific language refers to the primary assurance which words convey, with a linked succession of transfer of meaning. Imre Lacatos analyzed the relativity of scientific "progress" itself, since past "paradigms" (or "scientific research programs," as he himself defines them) may possibly be reactivated or retrospectively validated. A scientist's presuppositions (the methodological or experimental choices and starting points of his personal research) can hardly be described as rational or irrational, since the initial irrational reliance on intuitive ideas can lead to fruitful research.

This thesis was developed in a radical way by Paul Feyerabend, who adopted "methodological anarchism:" the epistemological tolerance of any methodological code and any scientific deontology, provided that research precedes them. More particularly, formal presuppositions of validity cannot be laid down in scientific language, since language reflects moments of inspiration and stimuli to research, tied to the personal culture of the researcher, and the dynamic of broader cultural, political and social change.

In the field of research in the natural sciences, the demand for a "linguistic positivism" retreated gradually before the widely affirmed impossibility of deriving from the way language works a firm methodological "objectivity" and diachronic validity. Research practice seems to adopt an epistemology which is less demanding in its requirements, returning to a practical and versatile linguistic semantics regardless of whether we can define the real linguistically.

The same is not true for the social sciences. The failure of "linguistic positivism" was followed by neoscholastic analyses of the function of language, chiefly marked by the attempt to assemble a body of intellective definitions of "pragmatic" coordinates of a "communicative logic" without any ontological foundation.

People want to express a "process rationality" which is contained as a given in daily communicative practice. But this communicative practice (*das kommunikative Handeln*) sidesteps the theoretical problems about the validity of rationality. The requirements for the codification of its "tool-like character" hint precisely at a "process" rationality. They are attempting to analyze these process presuppositions of rationality, and translate them into constitutional prescriptions of communicative practice: Prescriptions of "assent," of "subjective understanding," and finally of a functionalist "ethics of dialogue."

The "assent" is prescribed as an alternative to choosing between relativism and totalitarian demands. It is a "process" because bridging this polarization requires an inter-subjective evaluation of the utilitarian intentionality of communication and the usefulness of the evaluation constitutes the rationalistic intervention. With regard to the "inter-subjective understanding," it is sustained in the phenomenologically constituted (in a purely notional sense) practice of the "unforced inter-subjective coincidence of the will." This coincidence also concerns process because it is inter-subjective "according to circumstances" yet expresses a regulative dimension which renders it rational and not random. Finally the "morality of dialogue" is also a process in the degree in which the dialogue intervenes functionally to bridge the gap between "recognizing" and "benefiting." The dialogue function does not emerge from theoretical motives, nor does it obey a predetermined axiology, but is contained in the intentionality of the communication and accordingly constitutes a rationalist morality.

This schematic and excessively restricted summary of the problems of "communicative practice" fails to do justice to famous thinkers such as Habermas, Apel, Lyotard or Derrida. Nevertheless it perhaps suffices to convey the character or "climate" of an intellectual game centered on linguistic "transcendence," of an insistence on the separation of language from the universal fact of the *word*: the existential referentiality of the subject. Perhaps the most precious contribution of philosophers of "communication" is that their own writings demonstrate the non-coincidence of communication and language in modernity: Their expression is enclosed in a conception of "process" scientific method which undermines every possibility of communication. Writing is detached from the need to communicate, locating the social function of language in the process of instinctual collective self-preservation, rather than the experience and the struggle to participate in life through language.

The practical business of living in modern societies confirms the non-coincidence of communication and language. It is sufficient to mention as indicators common phenomena, such as:

- The replacement of language and conceptual discourse by the visual image. The image presents an individualistic consumer attitude. It imposes chosen visual stereotypes and a programmed flow of impressions. It subordinates linguistic meaning to iconic "information," to the usefulness of the "item of knowledge." It diverts language from expressing the experience of living.
- The contraction of the linguistic code of communication into hermetic idioms of professional specialization, or into a few hundred words which function simply as signifiers for large sections of the population.
- The dominance of the advertising model of the use of language. Language used for advertising methodically invalidates communicative logic, rational argument and the critical function of the understanding. It traps signifiers in associations that refer to desired objects signified, or to rejected appetites and demands.
- The transfer of the advertising model to the linguistic idioms of ideological, religious and political groups. These idioms create mutually exclusive domains of uniform communication with "a closed circle" of adherents. They are put together and function to impose or establish ready-made "convictions," and propose preset interpretations. They produced "wooden language," which conforms significance to type and minimizes understanding.

• The use of linguistic forms to express individual ideological identity without any intention of communication. A linguistic idiom is adopted for the ideological mobilization of the individual, his or her membership of a preordained group with some kind of individual distinctiveness. Imprisonment in the preset linguistic idiom is chosen to project subjective difference, but it precludes communication with whoever does not share the same linguistic stereotypes.

The separation of language from the power and inclination to communicate is not an invention of, or exclusive to, the modern age, but it is a distinguishing feature of modernity.

We say that language is an instrument and means of communication. But this instrument is assimilated and used by the individual as a subjective capability. Using this capability for communication presupposes the presence of a subjective disposition to communicate. Otherwise language serves to express the individual's demands, self-display or aggressiveness that have become autonomous and unrelated. Communication is always a struggle for individual self-transcendence.

In order for the individual to communicate he or she must want to understand what the other is saying, to discern "sense" in the words themselves and beyond the words, to advance from the signifiers to the experience of the things signified which the other wishes to express, to put himself or herself alongside the other's experience, that is, to understand it in distinction from his or her own experience, and consequently to withdraw radically from encapsulation in the certainties derived from his or her own individual experiences. It is in this sense that we say that linguistic communication is a struggle for individual self-transcendence.

The culture of modernity is an all-embracing way of life centered on the individual. For this reason language in modernity manifests the greatest historical decline as communication. It is preeminently the age of parallel monologues, of incompatible languages. And at the same time it is preeminently an age of the demand for "objectivity," of the demand for "a common logic," since the protection of the individual presupposes a utilitarian common understanding.

One could characterize modern times as the fullest and clearest historical realization of the myth of Babel. Perhaps no other age has invested such confidence in the communicative capabilities of linguistic logic, in the "common logic" of language or in the language of "common logic." And no other age has known such a tragic incompatibility between communication and logic.

Ideological versions of reality, scientific "schools" and research methods, techniques of analysis and systems of values, convergence of interests and group preferences create parallel and asymptotic linguistic codes, based on the rights of "self-determination," and "freedom of choice." Every linguistic code expresses a "well-grounded" logic, which destroys the communicative word. The logical defensive armor is derived from the self-evident principles of modernity, which are incompatible with the intention to communicate. Rationality is fragmented into as many kinds of defensive armor as there are forms of aggression and domination.

The word proves itself incapable of influencing life. Unreason pervades social, political, economic processes, shaping societies of uncommunicating individuals. Institutional "dialogues" and "consensual procedures" merely approve "pluralism," validating the destruction of the communicative word. "Pluralism" in modernity replaces the communicative word, without being a "common logic;" a range of subjectivities all lay claim to absolute "objectivity." Behind the impressive achievements of the good life for individuals lies an absence of community and a lack of concordance between communication and language.

4. The bankruptcy of ideologies

The transformation of life into ideology (the substitution of theory and organized aspiration for immediacy) is the basic mark of modernity. That is why the undermining of convictions and the widespread failure to satisfy desire experienced in contemporary societies is the most emphatic sign of the end of the modern age.

We have witnessed the collapse of sociopolitical regimes with a specific ideological identity, which vitally undermines the function of ideology. But doubtless it does not destroy it. The end of the ideologies indicates that we have now entered the postmodern age.

Collapse of fascist regimes, collapse of National Socialism, collapse of what was euphemistically called "existent socialism." But the collapse of the paradigmatic prototype of every later ideologico-social structure came first: the vital weakening of religious institutions in western societies, the widespread "religious fading" of the masses.

The transformation of the ecclesiastical reality in the Middle Ages spawned the modern type of ideology: the mutation of faith into individual conviction, rejecting the struggle to create social relations with the individual's reassuring submission to formal codes of behavior. One may trace the marks of all later ideological sociopolitical regimes from this paradigmatic institutionalization of ideological religiosity, and also their inevitable dynamic of collapse.

The first mark is the attempt to make ideology a social reality, translated into specific institutional blueprints for the functioning of the social whole. This necessitates the dogmatic codification of the ideology and the formation of a bureaucracy to impose it. Dogmatism becomes more widely acceptable when collective desire draws the illusion of certainty from it. Bureaucratic autocracy is effective if "convictions" can maintain the fantasy that desires are being fulfilled.

The second mark is militancy, the "missionary spirit" of ideology. Fidelity to dogmatic ideological principles is visible in the adherent's "missionary zeal;" wholehearted zeal presupposes a total submission to the institutional personification of the ideology. Recognizing the "infallibility" of the institutional leadership justifies this submission. Ideological faith collapses when individual needs prevail over the rapture sustaining a militant asceticism, or the satisfaction of the few thanks to the militancy of the many becomes painfully obvious.

The third mark is the transition from a society of communities to a society of totalitarian centralization, a mass society (or from catholicity as belonging to every local church to catholicity as worldwide expansion). This transition presupposes controlled structures of ideological homogeneity and "practical" conformity. Totalitarian centralization functions insofar as it satisfies the individual needs or illusory security which the ideology promises.

The fourth mark is the intellectualist pretensions of ideological "principles" (their apodictic or "scientific" foundation) and their progressive transformation into mysticism which is meta-rational and hyper-historical, but nevertheless possesses obligatory validity. The intellectualist arguments and their mystical derivatives collapse before the facts of experience and a demand for empirical verification.

Finally, the fifth mark is a retreat from radical reform or the progressive modernization which every ideology promises at inception, towards theoretical inflexibility, becoming incapable of self-analysis or self-criticism. Usually it is the "missionary" aim which inhibits any self-criticism leads gradually towards the psychological identification of the will of the followers with that of the leadership. The predominating irrationality of any ideology dresses itself up in a rationalism which can no longer perceive its own processes. The break between idealistic beginnings and a stagnant irrationality are fundamental internal contradictions which paralyze and undermine ideological systems.

This list of symptoms is episodic and impressionistic. Ideologies in modernity tend to replace ontological meaning by rational individual "conviction" and psychological identification with chosen forms of "efficiency" – ideological groups replace cohesive social bonds and the social dynamic created when ontological meaning is given to what really exists.

More particularly, the pursuit of "effectiveness" can easily lose contact with ideological convictions and presuppositions. Detaching the pursuit of effectiveness from systematic visions and theoretical promises may make ideological systems collapse. The entrepreneurial, technological management of the economy has proved incomparably more productive than any ideological economic logic. In an individual's life, the capacity to make use of "opportunities" has changed behavior much more than any faith in ideological blueprints for behavior.

In other words, ideologies collapse when confronted with instant gratification and the consumerist good life. The ontological void becomes apparent and any attempts to fill it with ideological convictions and organizational institutionalizations of desire are very rapidly exhausted. They concern only social minorities with old-fashioned attitudes.

Ideologies are abundant when the ontological understanding of human relations is replaced by the psychological preference for rationalistic relational schemes based on utilitarian principles. The ideologies asserted their own usefulness and sought to prove it "in a scientific fashion." Pursuing utilitarian results without intermediaries developed its own dynamic which outflanks ideologies and renders them superfluous. Modernity implies not only ideologies but also the autonomous pursuit of utility. The ideologies have peaked and collapsed at the same time.

The bankruptcy of ideologies has been accompanied by the collapse of faith in autonomous utilitarian beneficence. New aims and priorities suggest entry into the postmodern age, notably "quality of life" freed from the individualistic utilitarian understanding of human relations.

5. The developmental threat

The word "development" sums up the aspirations and ideals of the modern human person. Often synonymous with comfortable living, availability of consumer goods, freedom from toil, advanced social welfare, access to recreation, and the swift satisfaction of practical needs, "development" both defines and exhausts people's social aspirations.

The greatest possible exploitation of natural resources with constantly evolving technology and concomitant planning to benefit humankind is a more formal definition of "development."

"Development" is also the continual increase in the gross national product or in per capita production. All the relationships of production, consumption and exchange must be programmed to the structures and rhythms of an ever-increasing and more abundant productivity.

Putting "developmental" logic into practice causes radical social dislocation: transforming not only the economy but also political life, social behavior, mental outlooks, and hierarchies of values. Production is transferred from agriculture to industry, populations move to industrial regions, the countryside is abandoned and cities expand enormously. Knowledge and scientific research are tied to industry and the technological development of the means of production. The economy grows regardless of its social function and politics gives way to the needs of development.

Some symptoms which accompany development signs are valued as absolutely positive and others are denounced as manifestations of a unique kind of social and anthropological neobarbarism. Some of these signs constitute a real threat to the cultural continuity or even biological survival of the human race. Their threatening dynamic makes them distinctive signals for the collapse of a cultural "paradigm."

The first symptom is the inescapable drive, inherent in the logic of development, to exhaust energy sources and natural resources, the destruction of the biosphere and consequently of the prerequisites for the survival of the human species on earth. The "greenhouse effect," the destruction of the ozone layers of the atmosphere, the rapid shrinking of forests and the sea's plankton, the exhaustion of water resources, the pollution of seas and lakes, the increasing atmospheric pollution in the great conurbations, the periodic nuclear leakages, soil damage with chemical fertilizers, are only some of the ecological consequences of development.

But the logic of development is a pragmatic way of life, the obvious way to organize daily existence in developed societies, or a right to be demanded in "developing" countries. To save nature and assure the survival of the human species calls for an upheaval in the daily existence of many millions of people, radical changes in their way of life. For millions of the poor and destitute, it seems to end hope for an improvement in their condition of life and deliverance from suffocating privation and hardship. Sufficient motivation or persuasive proposals seem lacking for such a revolutionary voluntary break with the logic of development. The break presupposes a universal change of mentality, behavior and practice, a painful ascetic struggle for individual self-transcendence, the hierarchy of needs must be radically changed and life must be endowed with a different meaning. Liberating oneself from the logic of development implies the historical end of modernity and the entry into another cultural "paradigm." Any such event seems remote and improbable. Yet the danger for the natural environment, constitutes threats with a precise timetable.

Secondly, hidden totalitarianism is innate to the systematic developmental process.

Authoritarian regimes openly pursued "development" – at least in the case of Stalin and Mao. They interpreted it as a necessary phase to achieve a rapid transition from an agrarian to an industrial society.

But this undisguised totalitarianism, with its vast numbers of victims and nightmarish inhumanity, seemed less threatening because it claimed to be a mere tactic, ideologically and naively dressed up in an appeal to "historical necessity." The totalitarianism behind development presents an unlimited threat, precisely because it is hidden or dressed up in hedonism and the logic of development is incompatible with any limiting restraint.

If we call "totalitarianism" the imposition of discipline and control on human beings' social and private life, then the systematic claims of "development" are "totalitarian." Development processes, made autonomous by collective and individual choice, are necessary coordinates of eudaemonistic aspirations, hiding their totalitarian character, which is simply disguised. One may analyze many manifestations of eudaemonistic totalitarian power: Systematic propaganda for the masses in totalitarian regimes is replaced in "developed" societies by advertising. It assumes increasing consumption to be a self-evident goal, just as all totalitarian propaganda assumes the necessity of conformity with the prevailing ideology to be self-evident. To sustain the demand for increasing consumption, the individual submits to working overtime or taking an additional job. The rhythm of daily existence and private life conform to the centrally directed productive imperative. People's work burden creates the need for easy organized recreation: passive participation in predetermined forms of enjoyment, group vacations, and chiefly the daily abandonment of the self to television. Watching television transfers ready-made perceptions, ideas, convictions, calculated hierarchies of needs, priorities, interests and values methodically and imperceptibly.

The consumerist mentality also imposes political priorities: political programs are valued for the good life which they assure. Citizens weigh up their political choices according to the material benefits they might get. Setting aside material benefits carries a "political cost," that is, the loss of votes for the party or coalition which has not sufficiently addressed the consumerist mentalities. Priorities of social policy and long-term planning are ignored for instantly gratifying demands for material benefits under pressure from organized interests.

An authority set up to provide, and citizens who understand political action as a demand for material benefits create human dependency on "a maternal substance, a powerful archaic Mother." Relations of dependence seem to have been reversed – the voter is no longer tied to the patronage of the politician, but the politician is tied to the demands of his or her elective clientele. The manipulation of their demands, with the help of marketing techniques, subordinates the citizens' conscience and sensibility to a planned illusion of exchange.

To attain power, a party must offer the most persuasive illusion of imminent satisfaction of popular demands. The center of gravity of party political rivalry is transferred from comparing political programs to laying out eudaemonistic promises. Political life becomes a daily game of seducing the citizen in the realm of the fantastic, and the real elements of the common life are relegated to minority channels. What prevails is the game of images, of providing good television, of cajoling the citizen.

In "developed" societies, mass psychological manipulation is centered around television. Politics are played out on the small screen according to rules imposed by the need to produce images. The citizens do not gather to hear political speakers, to judge, to test, to refute. They are simply mute extras in the television spectacle, unwitting collaborators in their manipulation.

The destruction of the environment and the programmatic means to discipline people in uniform behavior, mentality and hierarchy of values accompany "development" like a law. This dynamic constitutes a manifest and immediate threat. For the first time in history, it is not limited geographically or to certain aspects of human life. The end of modernity may also be the end of human history on the planet or the return to an unimaginable primeval condition.

Prolegomena 3

The Lack Of Existential Meaning In Modernity

1. The meaninglessness of metaphysics and "fundamental confusions"

Questioning the cause and purpose, the reason or meaning, of human existence seems to be excluded in modernity.

The question raises awkward problems evoking historical associations of scientific backwardness, dogmatic priorities, ideological coercion, submission to illiberal institutions and authority. Modern humanity understandably reacts defensively, rejecting any approach beset with such associations.

The question raises methodological problems: modern theories of knowledge have no faith in rules for verifying non-empirical analyses. Whatever the semantic content of the cause and purpose, reason or meaning of human existence, they remain beyond the frame of reference of critical verification. Their interpretation is confined either to logical proof or sentimental persuasion. And for modern humanity's historical experience, abstract logical proof can only have a formal (that is, a conventional) validity. "Sentimental" is by definition non-rational and consequently beyond the scope of any consistent epistemological method.

The linguistic logic of modernity cannot endow existence with meaning. Signifiers of cause and purpose, the reason or meaning of existence, do not correspond to what is commonly accepted as signified and consequently cannot function as signs of practical communication. The semantic content of the words refers to underlying choices, attempts to *create* realities, not to *evoke* realities.

Ultimately, the meaning of existence appears to refer to the polarization between faith and science. The polarization has a clearly medieval origin, in the antithesis between fideism and intellectualism.[1] It refers to the epistemological dead-end reached with the individualistic investigation of possible knowledge, dividing truth-telling from communicating, and substituting the Greek *logos* of relations by the Latin subjective *ratio*.[2] From the beginning of the Western Middle Ages, *faith* lost its primary semantic content, which was *trust* or *confidence*, that is, the certainty of knowledge which is provided by the experiential immediacy of personal relationship. Faith was transformed into an individual mental "conviction," unrelated to either experience or the critical function of the mind.

Bacon, Hobbes, Kant and Jacobi treated this obvious polarization of faith and reason as a theory within the context of the Western European tradition.[3] To impose and consolidate this polarization socially and to trace it back to a common mentality underlie the modern "paradigm." Within this context, and in the mind of the average person, "science" is objectively verifiable and consequently universally valid knowledge, while the individual chooses "faith" for his or her metaphysical needs, without any requirement for analysis and proof.

The question concerning the cause, purpose, meaning or reason of human existence has to be transposed to the realm of faith, since objective verifiable answers are not forthcoming. Religious thinkers who attempt to construct a "science of the transcendent" come into sharp conflict with the modern demand for an experimental control of knowledge. Wittgenstein succinctly summarized the boundaries between the assumptions of apodictic science and the meaning of existence: "The sense of the world must lie outside the world. In the world everything is as it is and everything happens as it does happen: *in* it no value exists – and if it did exist, it would have no value. If there is any value that does have value, it must lie outside the whole sphere of what happens and is the case. For all that happens and is the case is accidental. What makes it non-accidental cannot lie *within* the world, since if it did it would itself be accidental. It must lie outside the world."[4]

The meaning of existence must therefore be sought outside the boundaries of the cosmos, that is, outside the boundaries of science – it becomes connected with faith. This metathesis is consequent on scientific logic and (especially in the case of Wittgenstein) preserves faith – empirically accessible but inexpressible (*unaussprechliches*) meaning of existence and of the cosmos, that which is higher (*das Höhere*) – from Western European philosophy's attempting for centuries to subject all things to the logic of a methodological homogeneity. By abandoning faith to its modern extra-empirical version, however, identified with an arbitrarily chosen personal "conviction," we also lose the meaning of existence (the "greater" realm of "the problems of life" – again Wittgenstein's expression[5]) to a vortex of "fundamental confusions:" confusions in regulative principles of human behavior, in the validity of institutions and structures, in the communicative use of reason, in the teleology of social reality, in how we judge human existence and human conduct.

The most fundamental confusion which modern faith creates lies in what Heidegger used to describe as the substitution of metaphysics by physics in the Western European tradition[6]: the "meta" physical meaning of nature is approached with concepts which function according to how the facts of nature are defined. The natural character of the metaphysical concept lies, of course, not in its interpretation as a natural fact, but in the way the signifiers define the concept, the manner in which natural facts become accessible to us.

In this perspective, words such as "God," "soul," "eternity" (signifiers of cause and aim, of metaphysical sustenance or potential of existence) refer to schematic definitions which do not correspond precisely to the representations of sensory perception. But they do presuppose the same mental reference to the definitive "constants" which are the basis of sensory perception: God is understood as "supreme being," "higher power," something much greater than sensible reality or sensory energy, something which cannot be measured yet exists fundamentally in the same mode as the things which can be measured. The soul is identified with the spiritual "part" or "element" of the individual, in contrast to the material and sensible, with the same positiveness which makes even what is perceptually individual and partial accessible. Eternity, too, is understood as a mental extension of the empirical knowledge of time, a broadening of the limits which define the uncircumscribable: a time which is infinitely extended but with definite divisions into historical periods.

To approach metaphysics with the conceptual assumptions of physics remains methodologically precarious and empirically unjustifiable. It is very easily undermined both as a consistent epistemological method and as empirical correspondence to human *desire*. And when we are speaking of *desire* in this context, we are lending to the term the pragmatic content of libido: the only impulse which (especially in human beings) transcends biological purpose and constitutes "an instinct of life, that is of immortal life, of irrepressible life, a life which has no need of organs, a life simplified and indestructible."[7] Both the demand for methodological validity and the primeval dynamic of desire are very difficult to reconcile with the logic of the definitive presuppositions which reduce metaphysics to physics.

The result is "fundamental confusions" in the "greater" realm of "the problems of life." The confusions are not confined to the religiosity of modern humanity. They do not lead simply to that new phenomenon in human history, the “religious fading” of the masses, to the psychological “rejection” of every existential and metaphysical question. The confusions go far enough to destroy the very ability to give meaning to human existence and human action. They confirm our assumption that life is irrational; they dissolve everything which is valid in the regulative principles of social life.

More specifically, from the point of view of the social consequences – which are more susceptible to a phenomenological approach – the lack of existential meaning in modernity is centered preeminently on the rejection of the problem of life after death, or the denial that it exists. It is no exaggeration to say that throughout the course of human history, reference to life after death is central to giving meaning to human existence and human action: Only if human existence survives the ephemeral biological cycle, and is extended beyond death, only then does responsibility for managing it transcend the demands of instinctual needs for survival. Only then can human actions have meaning, can they be obedient to regulative principles, since only then are the regulative principles not products of a conventional utilitarianism, but refer to ontological presuppositions for evaluating human behavior in the perspective of eternity.

If human existence ends with death, then it is wholly subordinate to biological goals, and does not differ in any way from the existence of any other species in the animal kingdom. The regulative principles of existence would in that case be simply biological imperatives: the impulses to self-preservation, pleasure, domination that are by definition antisocial. Individualism would clearly be legitimized, social relations justified only by their usefulness to the individual. The same would also be true even for the institutions of social life, the structures and working of the social conventions on which coexistence is based, the development of science and technology, spiritual culture and art. All have the utilitarian response to the instinctual demands of the ephemeral biological individual as their unique point of reference and exclusive principle of justification.

When the perspective of life after death is shut off from humanity, when self-awareness is confined simply to the limits of biological existence, then an awareness of the irrationality or madness of any non-utilitarian ethic and regulative principle, even of existence itself, inevitably emerges. The only basis of the natural uniqueness of humanity, its difference from the other species of the animal kingdom, is the blind necessity of biological evolution, synonymous with chance. And the unique end or goal of human existence is the satisfaction of the natural needs alone – biological and psychological – of the individual, the struggle for temporary survival.

But to identify the meaning of human existence with humanity's necessary subjection to biological randomness and the laws of nature implies the absence of sufficient reason for existence, that is, irrationality or absurdity. The culture of modernity presents us with a many-faceted expression of this absurdity, often dramatic and always perplexing. The so-called "art of the absurd" in its various manifestations, "nihilistic philosophy," or – in a progressive and timely way – the Nieztschean proclamation of "the death of God," have demonstrated with striking clarity the lack of existential meaning in modernity.

And this awareness of the absurdity of existence is not limited to the theorizing of intellectuals and artists. The absence of existential meaning is an obvious fact of our everyday existence: a gaping void underneath apparently trusting relationships, reliable words, sincere dispositions. If our existence is nullified by death, why should the individual restrain his or her instincts and appetites? Why should a professional person act ethically? Why should a businessman not be corrupt? Why should a judge or a public official not accept bribes? Why should a politician not misappropriate state revenue? Why should an employee serve the needs of the citizen? If human existence is a chance biological occurrence, what existential meaning and what regulative principle can prevail over instinct? What can inspire human beings to be just, unselfish, self-denying, creative, self-sacrificing on behalf of their fellows? What ethics or what logic could support them and justify such an attitude or effort?

At the beginning of the modern age, Enlightenment romanticism tried to conceal the lack of existential meaning by resorting to rationalism as if it were a natural demand. A human being is mere nature, but nature has an innate logic which guarantees living and self-preservation. Endowed by nature with the ability to discern and decipher the logic of nature, and function in a logical way, human beings need no other point of reference to deduce the meaning of their existence and the regulative principles of their behavior.

"Natural justice," the "natural rights of the individual," the rationalism of the "social contract" were impressive products of the Enlightenment's faith in the regulative principles derived from the natural rationality that replaces all metaphysical foundations of morality. Even the political theories of the modern age, the objectives and programs of social ideologies, whether of free or regulated economic systems, pacifist and ecological movements, reflect this very faith in natural rationality and its regulative usefulness.

Nevertheless, as we have seen in the preceding pages, natural rationality as a regulative principle was not without contradictions and insurmountable problems. Let us recall that the Enlightenment found evidence for the rationality of nature in cosmic harmony, order and functionality. It also assumes, however, as presuppositional principles, a strict legalism, a relentless determinism and a programmatic intentionality. Thus the rationality of nature, as a regulative principle, demands that human beings submit to a new transcendent, impersonal authority. It leaves no real margins of freedom and existential otherness to the human subject, nor is it propitiated by any kind of "piety."

Not only do the harmony and order of the universe arise from the logic of nature, but also the priority of the biological urge towards self-preservation, violent instinct, the drive towards dominance and power, the right of the strongest, the insatiable pursuit of pleasure. In an oblique fashion with La Mettrie and straightforwardly with the Marquis de Sade, we are told in great detail – still within the context of the Enlightenment – that "so-called evil is the way nature works," while "so-called virtue arises only as a denial of nature and from the struggle against nature, and thus in either case has no meaning." Crime itself "is rooted in the biological structure of humanity, can in itself provide enjoyment, because it comes forth from the voice of nature within humanity and serves the enlargement of individual power and also in certain circumstances the maximizing of pleasure."[9]

Who, then, can persuade somebody convinced of the ephemeral nature of human existence to accept as the regulative principle of his or her life the first and not the second version of natural rationality, and with what criteria: to accept the discipline of rational nature expressed in the harmony and order of relationships, and not the violence of instinct and the unrestrained pursuit of pleasure, which are equally natural but destructive of relationships? Confronted with imminent annihilation through death, only a utilitarian and hedonistic expediency can guide one in choosing between either version of natural rationality.

It is of course possible for an individualistic utilitarian expediency to inspire useful contracts to regulate collective behavior, but they are inevitably relative and precarious. The relativity of every kind of morality – the reliance on the relativity of laws and customs according to time and place – is one of the most widely popularized and emphatically projected theses of the Enlightenment. And it is this relativity which makes impossible the construction of universally acceptable regulative principles drawn from natural rationality.

The culture of modernity is perhaps the unique example in human history of such generalized passive acceptance of strident contradictions, of making contradictions socially obvious:

A culture which is organized and functions around an absolute tool-like rationalism, while at the same time denouncing, in both progressive theoretical thought and artistic expression, the absurdity and tyranny of mechanistic rationality.

A culture which is founded on a most consistent materialism, and raises nature to the supreme level as the causal principle of existence and as a regulative authority, while at the same time it justifies and gives systematic expression to the most undisguised intervention in the laws and the logic of nature, it violates nature and treats the functional modesty of nature licentiously for the sake of an extremely risky, reckless and shortsighted utilitarianism.

A culture which aspires to being – and really is – radically anthropocentric, militantly anti-metaphysical, and inimical to any ontology, supposedly to liberate humanity from submission to restrictive dogmas and institutions invested with excessive authority. A culture which struggles almost hysterically to give humankind an absolute value, to safeguard the individual's freedom and equality of rights, to abolish the humiliations to which people are subjected as a result of racism and class and social inequalities. Yet at the same time this very culture obstinately cultivates a faith in the inescapable nothingness and the absurdity or meaninglessness of human existence, in the exclusively biological interpretation of humankind as an advanced link in the evolutionary chain of species, in the aleatory and random nature of humanity's spiritual gifts. A culture which labors to prove beyond doubt that matter under certain conditions produces spirit, that humanity derives its origin from pithecoids, that intelligent beings exist on other planets, consequently stripping humanity of any nobility and lofty existential uniqueness.

In these strident contradictions, which are so thoroughly assimilated to the mentality of modern humanity, the question of the cause and purpose, the reason or meaning of human existence leads inevitably to "fundamental confusions," or is referred to meaningless chance and coincidence. Whatever attempts have been made to find, in spite of all this, some universally accepted point of reference, from which regulative principles of collective social life and individual behavior may be drawn – such as "communicative" usefulness, or rational effectiveness, or the dynamic of "hope" for a more just and more happy "world order" – they have proved to be utopian or comically naïve. In particular, the rational effectiveness invested in the messianic promises of totalitarian systems which have so marked the twentieth century, has also tragically disappointed modern humanity: the shame and horror of scientifically systematized violence, policed consciences, the impoverishment or even destruction of millions of human existences for the sake of ideological goals.

Only the philosophy of existentialism, particularly its French version, has proved radically consistent enough to demonstrate the absurdity of existence while proposing something to endow this absurdity with meaning. Nihilism, for French existentialism, is the deepest foundation and the inescapable end-point of existence, yet the human being is the only thing that exists which has the capacity to annihilate its nihilism through its consciousness and its acts which are in the process of becoming. Consciousness constantly expands existence by its very being: it summarizes existence as that which can come to be at any moment, annihilating the past which represents its being. The ontological foundation of human existence is the self-annihilation of its being, that is, life as "facticity" (*facticité*), as the destruction of every definitive identity. Only the human person can be that which it is not, and not be that which it is. For the human person "is that which it does," the potentiality of action precedes and annihilates the being-itself of the definitive "essence" of the human person. The human being is "cast out" (*jeté*) into the midst of the absurdity of the transitory and the fortuitous, but within the *praxis* of life it can sketch out its own contours, recognizing that beyond these contours nothing exists, and that their being sketched out in *praxis* is limited every moment to "a useless passion." To live the absurd, creating to the limit (historically or artistically), filling the meaningless void with beauty and hope: this is a kind of "heroic despair," a "holiness without God," an absolute and tragic faith in humanity which wishes to cohabit with the dynamic of the meaning of existence, to function as a noble and disappointed ethical stance.

The question is whether this proposition can serve to endow human existence and activity with meaning. In spite of the arresting ontological problem which it implies,[10] there is something lacking not only about the motives and the goal of such "heroic" despair, but more especially with regard to the social functionality of the proposition: Because the proposition does not cease to be asphyxiatingly egocentric, abandoning the dynamic of social relations neglected for egotistic choices for sketching out the subjective "contours," or for the illusory ideological blueprints for such "planning." Moreover, the otherness of subjective becoming can be the cause or effect of the dynamic of social relations, but it is still rooted in the absurdity of the ephemeral and its origin in the fortuitous, and therefore is exhausted as simple phenomenology which excludes by definition the construction of existential meaning.

The endeavor of existential philosophy has proved clearly

that the cause and purpose, the meaning or reason of human existence remain altogether incomprehensible on the basis of a nihilistic ontology. And that within the modern "paradigm" there is no epistemological method or linguistic logic to construct an ontology which would neither surrender to inexplicable nihilism nor be tied to the assumptions of medieval non-empirical intellectualism or to a Newtonian submission of metaphysics to each successive human interpretation of nature. To understand what exists and is real and endow it with meaning is a dilemma that modernity cannot resolve: Either we resort to random and aleatory irrationality, that is, to a simple phenomenicity which corresponds only to the absence of existential meaning, or we return to an ontology of "mental images" insisting on a medieval intellectualism or on a Newtonian "representational" theory of knowledge.

Obviously when modern Newtonian epistemology attempts metaphysical etiologies, it ends up with an ontology of "mental images" too. It differs from medieval intellectualism only in respect of the "representational" or "re-representational" priorities which it posits and accepts as empirical. To attain knowledge of reality on the basis of this idea presupposes necessarily the "immobilization" of the dynamic of becoming in specific "constants" which mostly need mathematical-quantitative definitions if they are to be articulated. And the attractive advantage of the "representational" method is to offer humanity the satisfaction and assurance of possessing knowledge by more than an abstract comprehension. It must have valid and positive knowledge of reality, since it can transcribe it into constant "signifiers" which coordinate in the same way every subjective intellection, guaranteeing the "objectivity" of knowledge. People believe that they have knowledge of reality by means of its semiological transcription, receiving the data of reality as objects which they empower from the moment when they can define them "objectively." This is the logic which assures authoritative dominion over reality, but it is a "representational" logic, which is verified by the utilitarian exploitation of definitively signified reality.

Nevertheless, ontological attempts at endowing existence with cause and meaning, which have relied on the use of the "representational" method,[11] have resulted in a dubious metaphysics of "mental images."[12] And the nihilistic ontology of empirical phenomenology which aspired to dethrone it left manifestly unanswered the question of cause and aim, the logic or the meaning of existence. The presuppositions and potentialities of these two propositions to make sense of the existent and the real seem to exhaust the modern "paradigm." Only in the "apophatic" language and unorthodox methodology of post-Newtonian physics does a radically different epistemological and hermeneutic approach to the existent and the real begin to emerge. If this methodology and language can also articulate a proposition that gives meaning to the existent, then it also signals entry into the postmodern age.

2. The new coordinates of the void

Modernism gave nihilistic ontology two powerful authoritative supports. Both broaden its social repercussions and characterize the mentality of the modern human being. I am referring to two new propositions about what exists and is rational: a proposition about the *random* creation of what exists and another about the evolutionary emergence of what is rational. The reality of the *unconscious*, an essential factor in the interpretation of the rational distinctness of the human being, also plays a subordinate role.

All three elements of the ontological problem refer to the assertions or "working hypotheses" of scholarly research. In the climate, however, of the ideological priorities of modernity they are very rapidly popularized, appropriated as arguments of militant materialism, and help refute any metaphysic and any meaning of the existent and the rational.

Chance, as the causal principle of what exists, is not a hermeneutic proposition exclusive to the modern age. Even in antiquity the view was sometimes held that matter was eternal and that it was its chance (or automatic) combinations that led to the formation of the world. Nevertheless – at least in the impressive cases of Heraclitus, Democritus and the Epicureans – this version functions rather as a necessary condition of other hermeneutic assumptions for the clarification of cosmic becoming.[13] It does not constitute a carefully worked out proposition or indicate systematic inquiry into the causal principle of what exists. And moreover, we can also find in these philosophers a view of chance which refers unambiguously to metaphysical entities (deities, soul, transcendence of the good, etc).

Neither in antiquity nor in the medieval period do we have evidence or proof that the invocation of chance led to a nihilistic ontology analogous to modernity's. Nor did it constitute a particular cosmological theory, or an ideological current of wider social acceptance. It is hard to judge how philosophical theses are reflected in society. Nevertheless the written sources suggest that the Aristotelian discussions of chance both reflected and shaped a centuries-long widespread and self-evident familiarity.

Aristotle established and clarified the semantic contrast between the terms "chance" (*tychê*) and "nature" (*physis*). Nature is always identified with a programmatic intentionality and is a concept that does not coincide with chance.[14] Thus the fortuitous manifests only the undetermined nature of accidents or the undetermined nature of choice.[15]

Such a discussion – and by extension the tracing back of all contingent being and of the universe itself to a causal principle – appears to be self-evident also within the framework of the philosophical systems of Platonism, Stoicism and Neoplatonism, which together with Aristotelianism prevailed from the early classical period to the end of the Middle Ages. It would not be perverse of us to conclude that this common philosophical position – a common presuppositional principle of interpretation of the world – shapes and reflects a broader social mindset.

It is characteristic that in the long period of dramatic contrast and fermentation which pervaded the Greek and non-Greek world following the appearance of Christianity, the nonexistence of a causal principle of existence and consequently the nonexistence of God are problems never raised. Christianity does not come to proclaim and prove the existence of God to a world which doubts or is ambivalent about it. Christianity poses a problem for Greek thought: the possibility of linking a theoretical certainty about a causal principle with the immediacy of historical experience and relationship of humanity with a *personal* God – a problem of real-existential (and not simply conceptual) communion of the created with the uncreated.

The first historical attempts to furnish proofs for the existence of God appear in Western European scholasticism, that is, when the terms of Greek epistemological theory and Early Christian ontology were radically overturned.[16] It is not that these arguments always existed and that new social factors and intellectual issues stimulated recourse to "proofs" of the existence and causal principle of the world. It was the epistemological presuppositions and utilitarian priorities of scholasticism that led necessarily to the "proofs:" methodological consistency and the imposition of theological intellectualism presupposed them.

The intellectualist "proofs," however, also opened up the way to the intellectualist doubting of the "proofs." Making rationalist affirmations autonomous also inevitably made rationalist denials autonomous. According to Heidegger, the "death of God" in modernity emerges inescapably from the "inner logic" of Western European metaphysical intellectualism.[17] An autonomous intellectualism trapped metaphysics in the presuppositions of a worldly physical rationality, elevating this rationality to new bases for metaphysics. Modernity had only to discard such axiomatic elevation to accept rationality as an absolutely this-worldly principle of how existence works.

The problem of a causal principle was thus either discarded as incompatible with positive verification, or was referred to the natural rationality of the probable, that is, to the random and the aleatory. The logical inadequacy of doing this manifestly violated natural rationality itself, but did not hinder the broadest popularization of faith in causal chance. The ideological agenda for the modern age found the principle of chance an exceptionally useful *a priori* starting point, which worked well in the mythopoeic dynamic of ideology.

Chance, as cause of what exists, was also offered as hermeneutic explanation for the first appearance of living matter. When chemistry was able to analyze the constitution of a living cell and the structure of organic substances, the transition from inorganic to organic substances as also the result of coincidental circumstances, of chance conditions, appeared rational and self-evident. Here, too, the logical inadequacy and the lack of scientific evidence for accepting this automatic transition from lifeless to living matter did not hinder its broad popularization.

The leap from non-rational to rational existence, the difference between human and animal life, remained difficult to interpret. It received clarification from the popularized theory of Darwin, inserting evolutionary theory into a materialist ideology. The spiritual capabilities of the human person were interpreted as products of an exclusively cerebral function and the primitive human brain as a consequence of the evolutionary process. Once again, scientific evidence and logical consequence were lacking, but the mythopoeic dynamic of ideology on the social level neutralized the demand for rational and research-based proof. The principle that "under certain conditions matter produces spirit" functioned and still functions as one of the basic focal points of modernity's ideological priorities. The chance generation-formation-function of the universe, the automatic generation of animate matter with innate evolutionary blueprints, the evolutionary production of spirit from matter: these are the new ontological theories which modernity introduces. In spite of their logical shortcomings and the inadequacy of scientific evidence, even for such arbitrary ideologies, these theories shape the ontological perspective of the modern person and give meaning to the modern *mode* of life. For this reason they cannot be ignored in any attempt to represent the ontological question as a problem about real life.

These theories, centered on an absolutely endocosmic hermeneutic of the existent and the real, a hermeneutic denying any metaphysical "meaning," also radically reappraise the method and language of ontological questions. After the endocosmic ontology of modernity, in order for the ontological question to be posed as a problem relevant to everyday life, it must be separated from the associations of its Western European philosophical prehistory: It cannot be posited without empirical language and method, or with the abstract categories and forms of formal logic.

Not that the empirical priority abolishes the logical, which alone can form, note and communicate experience. But it does prevent logical proof from being autonomous, detaching it from experience. If, then, the ontological question seeks a proposition which gives meaning to human existence and to human action, a proposition which contributes to the common empirical approach, its language and method should be purged not only of the intellectualist self-sufficiency of the European past but also of the ideological arbitrariness of modernity.

After chance and evolutionary theory, the reality of the unconscious is the third new element of the ontological problem brought into being by modernity. If the appearance of quantum mechanics with its principle of indeterminacy radically changed our understanding of the physical world and our approach to it, an analogous role has arguably been played in anthropological research by the detailed study of the unconscious.

The phenomenology of the conscious events and manifestations of the human psyche are inadequate to explain the reality of humanity's *being*, and especially the spiritual functions which constitute humanity's existential particularity. Consciousness defines only one partial "region" in the much broader and more complex "territory" of psychic life, while subjectivity is also formed and functions on "levels" of psychic life which are pre-conscious and non-conscious: Things suppressed from the conscious mind, which activate desires, unacknowledged subjection to social demands, indelible experiences shrouded in darkness, unclarifiable urges, imaginary substitutes for reality, infantile experiences which have never been made conscious, etc., etc.

The experiential and experimental study of these "levels" concentrates not on a static and passive "substratum" or "deposit" of experiences of the psyche, but on an active factor in the functioning of psychic life. The unconscious factor intervenes actively and decisively influences the formation and function of subjective existence.

The role of the unconscious in the active constitution of the subject demonstrates how undetermined the subject remains, how little subject to objectivization. To recognize the indeterminacy of the subject dissolves Cartesian illusions, identifying subjectivity with self-conscious thought, and the self-affirmation of existence from thought – illusions in large part sustaining the supposedly positivistic structure of modernity.

In particular the Lacanian (from Jacques Lacan and his school) contribution to the investigation of the unconscious, the demonstration of its *referential* composition and structure, obliges us to carry out a radical review of the problem of the *hypostasis* of the human person: The reality of the subject is not exhausted by its psychosomatic energies, which only constitute the *mode* in which the subject operates existentially. Already, Freudian analysis referred to an indefinable nucleus (*Kern*) of hypostatic subjectivity, a nucleus preceding even the unconscious, which we recognize, however, only when manifested and labeled as the *mode* of the word. Words form the subject as existential fact not only as consciousness but also as the unconscious. The unconscious itself "is structured like a language."[18] Both what is structured and its subject are analogous to language – language as the totality of signifiers and the marshaling of things signified – that is to say, the fact of reference and relationship.

The reality of the unconscious imposes indefinable anthropological terms which do not lend themselves easily to ideological popularization. On the contrary, the unconscious undermines mechanistic explanations of the workings of the psyche and frustrates the exclusive reference to neurophysiology.

In this way, the ideological exploitation of the reality of the unconscious has tended more to doubt autonomy and freedom, not only as that which distinguishes humanity from any other living existence, but also as the necessary prerequisite for regulative-moral principles. If both our willing decisions and rational judgments depend more or less on unexamined unconscious assumptions and influences, then our moral values are clearly relativized and our free will may be only an idealistic illusion.

The ideological exploitation of how research into the unconscious puts a question mark over freedom and morality (the subject's freedom of existential self-definition, morality's link to existential authenticity and fulfillment), in spite of the logical inadequacy of arbitrary schematization, promotes the nihilistic ontology of modernity, and intensifies the lack of existential meaning. The reality, however, of the unconscious is trapped within the intentionalities of the ideological construct in an incomparably more problematic way than are the metaphysics of chance or evolutionary theory. The primary importance of the unconscious is as a new ontological constituent in anthropological study, a datum which cannot be ignored.

Parenthesis 1

THE "LOGICAL PLACE"[1] OF CHANCE

1. If the sense of the world exists it must lie outside the world.[2]
2. If the sense of the world does not exist, if the world is senseless and irrational, then reality is found only within the world and is absolutely inexpressible. Then all that happens within the world and is the case can be verified, but not be expressed. The meaninglessness of the world is not susceptible of expression because expression would constitute meaning. If reality is absolutely this-worldly it is also absolutely senseless.
3. If the world is without sense and inexplicable, only then can it be the result of chance. Chance fundamentally reflects an accident-coincidence to which questions of causality ("whence?") or mode ("how?") or object-purpose ("for what?") cannot be put. That is to say, what has come about by chance is not subject to the constitutive elements of meaning. For this reason the fortuitous is also synonymous with the senseless and the inexplicable.
4. The world as a product of chance is a contradictory proposition. It proposes the inexplicable as an explanation. It interprets non-sense as sense.
5. As a hermeneutic "principle" of the world, chance is a contradictory but intelligible proposition. It attributes the generation and forming of matter, its evolutionary changes, the activated functionality of the world, to

unexplained accidents and nonsensical coincidences. It attempts to construct meaning while abolishing the constitutive elements of meaning. It is an intelligible proposition, but without a "logical place" and for this reason is nonsensical. It is a pseudo-proposition.

6. The fortuitous lays claim to the logical space of the probable, the logic of probability: From an infinity of possibilities the world arises by accident and functions by coincidence. But the very infinity of possibilities lends probability such a minimal value that it cannot prevail as a hermeneutic principle (it excludes the logico-mathematical content of probability).
7. The generation and formation of the world, as "exemplary place" of probabilities, includes an infinity of possibilities with the same degree of probability. Possible different indications are: the first fluctuations of temperature; the quantitative similarities between the initial facts (photons, electrons and neutrons); the pattern of like and unlike forms in the radiation of energy; the indices of the rhythm of the expansion of the universe; the fluctuations in density; the quantities of radiation or absorption of photons by electrons; the power and properties of nuclear forces; the relationship between electromagnetic forces and gravity; and the values of universal constants.[3]
8. In the theory of probabilities we mark the limits: certain, possible, impossible.[4] When the ratio of one particular accident to the possibilities of accident is one to infinity, it is impossible to explain the accidental by the probable. A probability amongst infinities may not be logically impossible, but it is logically impossible for it to be a hermeneutic proposition.
9. "The minimal unit for a probability proposition is this: The circumstances [...] give such and such a degree of probability to the occurrence of a particular event."[5] For the logic of probabilities to function, particular cir-

cumstances and existential facts subject to a number of variables are presupposed. Accidents and coincidences appearing before the generation and formation of coincidental facts and circumstances transcend the logical place of a probability proposition.

10. A monkey striking the keys of a typewriter at random can probably eventually produce one of Shakespeare's poems. It is, however, impossible as a probability for Shakespeare's poem to be produced without the pre-existence as facts of the monkey and the typewriter.
11. If the universe has a beginning in time, the logic of probabilities cannot explain this beginning. Which means that the fortuitous and accidental, as a function of the probable, cannot be a causal principle of the universe before circumstances existed to give this or that degree of probability to the realization of the actual universe.
12. As a causal and functional "principle" for the world, chance is a hermeneutic principle as nonsensical as any mythical explanation of the world.
13. There are only two intelligible hermeneutic propositions about reality: That the world has meaning, or that the world is the product of chance. These propositions attribute the generation and formation of matter-energy, and its evolutionary configurations, the way the activated world works (where lines of cause are finally traced back) to deliberate or chance conditions and possibilities. They refer back to the "principle" of intentionality (of meaning), or to the "principle" of chance (of the senseless) which governs the world. Both "principles" are intelligible, but only the former defines a place in logical space.
14. As a hermeneutic proposition of the causal principle of the world, chance has zero logical space. As a hermeneutic proposition of the functional principle of the world, it is simply tautologous, and therefore destructive of any

hermeneutic content. It tells us that all things that occur and are the case occur and are the case by a coincidental accident. It allows no logical space for questions and consequently none for answers.

15. The logical space of intentionality is indefinable. As a hermeneutic proposition of both the causal and the functional principle of the world, intentionality poses meaningful questions – which are the constitutive elements of its logical space. Thanks to intentionality, the whole of the logical space of the world becomes a meaningful question, a question extended into all possible situations of things. For this reason the logical space of intentionality is indefinable.
16. Uncircumscribed, the logical space of intentionality establishes and perpetually maintains philosophy and science. As zero logical space, chance destroys philosophy and makes science nonsensical.
17. Chance differs from indeterminacy. The two propositions are fundamentally distinct. As a hermeneutic proposition, indeterminacy refers to specific regions of reality: to sub-atomic space and to the biosphere. It says that in these regions the order of activated facts is not predictable: the activated fact has an unpredictable property, in harmony always with certain first principles but not constituted by these principles.
18. Indeterminacy is a hermeneutic principle with meaning: It refers to the *whence* and *how* and *for what* of specific facts. But it does not bind the constitutive elements of its logical space to firm causal structures which predetermine the explanation of the fact. It recognizes in the probabilistic character of the factors constituting the fact the *how* or the mode of its accomplishment. The same factors and natural parameters constitute the given and causal *whence*. And the functionality of the fact constitutes the final *for what*.

19. The principle of indeterminacy gives meaning to the unpredictable, to otherness, and recognizes the non-predetermined dynamic of *relationship* as an existent category. It postulates the unpredictable as a sufficient condition for the stability of the structures of the micro-cosm and the functional cohesion of cells and organisms.[6] The indeterminacy of the relations between cause and effect serves (and explains) the final functionality of the effect. The unpredictable serves the functional intentionality; freedom of choice constitutes a causal principle of physical teleology.
20. Indeterminacy is a proposition at the opposite pole to chance. In the probabilistic behavior of the factors of sub-atomic space or of the molecular formation of the cell, the proposition of indeterminacy recognizes not an event of accidence-coincidence-chance, but a free regulative principle of the functionality of effects, an endogenous "cybernetic" activity (Monod).

Parenthesis 2

The "Logical Place" Of The Theory Of Evolution[1]

1. If the sense of the world exists it must lie "outside" the world.[2] If the world has no sense, then even the question concerning the existence or nonexistence of meaning must make its appearance under severely endocosmic presuppositions. The theory of evolution is a proposition that interprets these presuppositions.
2. The posing of a question about the sense of the world presupposes the function of thought and symbolic expression. Thought and symbolic expression are aspects of reality which we describe as "spiritual" and refer to "the human spirit." Evolutionary theory says that the human spirit does not constitute a discontinuity in the evolution of living beings.
3. If the evolution of living beings is defined by strictly endocosmic (or materialist) criteria, then the point of departure of the phenomenon of evolution, the appearance of living beings, should also be defined by the same criteria. The theory of evolution says that matter under certain conditions produces life and that animate matter under certain conditions produces spirit.
4. The final conditions under which animate matter produces spirit are located, for the purpose of evolutionary theory, in the function of the brain. Accordingly, we encounter some spiritual manifestations (chiefly memory,

senses, exercise of choice, communication) in many life forms which possess advanced brains.

5. The quantitative and qualitative differences of the spiritual powers of human beings must, in this perspective, be attributed to the evolution of the genetic blueprints in the human brain – to specific endocosmic conditions of the "recording" of the spirit in the genetic code of human beings.
6. According to the theory of evolution, the conditions for "recording" a developed spirit in the human genetic code must be imposed by the instinct of self-preservation. A necessary condition for self-preservation was humanity's accommodation to the laws of the cohesion of the group (laws of the "tribe"). Adaptation to these laws was a condition of the survival of the fittest and over a long period exercised a decisive influence on the evolution of genetic blueprints for the human brain.
7. This proposition attributes to the evolution of the brain's genetic blueprints the brain's ability to safeguard by intellectual constructs the human need to adapt to the laws of group cohesion. These necessary intellectual constructs produced in an evolutionary fashion the mythical interpretations of the laws of the tribe, the religious interpretations of the myths, and the philosophical interpretations of religion. From this complex of evolutionary ideas the question arises of the sense of the world.
8. Within the perspective of an exclusively materialist evolutionary theory, the question about the sense of the world is written into humanity's genetic code, a product of the needs of adaptation to group symbiosis, a product of biological particularity for humanity's self-preservation.
9. In the hermeneutic logic of evolutionary theory other hermeneutic propositions are also posited. The "disputed area" between evolutionary theory and rival hermeneutic

propositions is delineated by the discontinuity of evolution from inanimate to animate matter and from brain function to specifically human spiritual abilities.

10. In this disputed area the theory of evolution lays claim to the logical space of the probable, the logic of probabilities – principally in whatever concerns the emergence of animate matter. In some primeval phase of the transformations of matter, in the particular conditions of planet earth and nowhere else in the billions of astral bodies, certain inanimate chemical elements under the random influence of electromagnetic changes, suddenly contravene the laws of chemistry[3] and form organic structures, that is, a new material reality by its constitution and operation which is compatible only in a functional sense with the second law of thermodynamics of cosmic becoming, the law of entropy.
11. "Whatever the composition of the primeval soup (assuming, of course, that it did not already contain living beings), and whatever the prevailing conditions, the probability of an original 'spontaneous' fluctuation transforming fragments of matter into complex organic compounds, which thereafter passed into proto-life forms capable of almost simultaneously inventing the servomechanisms of metabolism and replication, a genetic code that works only if the products embodying its translated instructions are already available, a permeable or impermeable membrane as occasion requires – such a probability is small to vanishing point."[4]
12. Just as infinitesimally small is the probability that organic matter can balance functionally, by coincidence during two or three billion years, the second law of thermodynamics, or the law of entropy: "Everything happens as if life, though certainly not violating the second law of thermodynamics, is indefinitely shortchanging it, avoiding it, making it irrelevant to its operations. One might

compare this to a gambler, who in the course of a marathon game of roulette has placed his stakes some 10^{100} times and so knows how to combine his stakes and bets that, though he started with a penny, he has now amassed a billion billion tons of gold (these numbers are not simply figures of speech), and is still winning."[5]

13. It should be added that in the "paradigmatic space" of this game of chance not a single instance of bad luck occurs, that is to say, no reversal towards an increase of entropy. The only question is this: "What are we to say about this constant rise over the last two billion years against the downward slope of entropy, about this growing (and, it seems, accelerating) complexification not only of species but of the biosystem as a whole? What are we to say of the increase each time by bounds to the power of ten, in the order and interdependence of the properties of its parts? Or that in 10^{16} successive seconds there has never been a spontaneous, important and lasting downward fluctuation in the system capable of pushing it, even temporarily, towards its natural downward slope?"[6]
14. The random and accidental genesis of animate matter does not provide the theory of evolution with logical space. When the relationship of one particular accident to the different possible accidents is one to infinity, the accident cannot be explained by probability. One probability amongst an infinity of probabilities may not be logically impossible, but it is impossible for it logically to constitute an adequate hermeneutic proposition.[7]
15. The theory of evolution also claims the logical space of the inductive conclusion: The universality and continuity of evolution becomes logically obligatory when the cases of continuity are much more frequent than those of discontinuity. The cases of continuity cover the "micro-evolutions," that is, the transition by stages from one species to another that is related to the former (wolf

- dog). The cases of discontinuity are confined to "macro-evolutions," that is, to abrupt transition from one type of organism to another, e.g. from amphibians to reptiles, or from reptiles to birds, when completely new types of organs and systems make their appearance. A great leap of discontinuity, e.g. the sudden appearance of the most delicate mechanism of the eye, constitutes the "transition" from eyeless invertebrates to vertebrates endowed with eyes, without any trace of an intermediate stage.

16. The logical validity, however, of an inductive conclusion is precarious and vulnerable, when the general conclusions arise from atomic or partial propositions which are not all verified. In particular in subatomic space and in the biosphere, the principle of indeterminacy completely excludes any application of the inductive method.[8] More generally, in modern epistemology the validity of the inductive method is doubted even when general conclusions can be traced back to partial or atomic propositions which are all positively verified.[9] The obligatory derivation of definitive universal principles from partial propositions binds scientific research to dogmatic certainty about its conclusions, which cuts it off from the fruitfulness that results from doubting what is clear and self-evident.
17. The contradictory linking of entelechy and chance, while defining the presuppositions of the evolutionary process, creates a vast gap in the logical space of the theory of evolution. Although the transition from inanimate to animate matter is regarded as random, the product of this random event appears from the outset to come with an immutable (for billions of years) genetic program written into its structure – "provided during all that time with powerful molecular control networks guaranteeing its functional coherence."[10]
18. If we maintain that *a priori* chance possesses entelechy

and that innate intentionality is random, we nullify the logical space of our assertion: "Propositions show what they say: tautologies and contradictions show that they say nothing."[11]

19. The logical space of the theory of evolution is judged on the continuity or discontinuity of development from animal brain function to specifically human spiritual powers. The quantitative and qualitative difference between the spiritual powers of human beings and the consequences of animal brain function poses problems concerning the logical consistency of the comparisons and the hermeneutic adequacy of the etiologies.
20. A first query about the logical consistency of the hermeneutic comparisons uses the given weakness in controlling the terms of the comparison epistemologically: "A logician might remind the biologist that his efforts to 'understand' the complete functioning of the human brain are doomed to fail, since no logical system can produce an integral description of its own structure. [...] [T]his logical objection does not apply to the analysis by man of the central nervous system of an animal, a system which may be supposed to be less complex and less powerful than our own. But even in this case a major difficulty remains: an animal's conscious experience is and no doubt will always be impenetrable to us."[12]
21. We estimate that the most advanced brain of a pithecoid has about five billion neurons. The human brain, however, has between fifty and a hundred billion. The neurons are linked to each other through synapses, amounting to between ten and twenty thousand per neuron. The "epigenetic development of a structure as complex as the central nervous system," limits us, in spite of the impressive progress of neurophysiology and electrophysiology, to a "profound ignorance concerning the fundamental mechanisms of the central nervous system."[13]

22. The impressive progress of neurophysiology and electrophysiology has told us a lot about where the receiving, transmitting, coordinating, retaining and retrieving of the (mainly sensory) stimuli of encephalic activity are situated. Nevertheless "we are still a long way from an interpretation of synaptic transmission in terms of molecular interaction."[14] We know *what* is accomplished in an area of encephalic activity and *where* it is accomplished. But we do not know *how* it is accomplished. We are therefore unable to formulate an adequate hermeneutic proposition.
23. The placing of these functions of the central nervous system permits a certain phenomenological comparison between the "performances of the neuron" and the performances of a computer. But "we must note that, at present, the parallel is confined to the lower levels of integration: the initial stages of sensory analysis, for example. The higher functions of the cortex, which achieve expression through language, seem to elude such methods of approach."[15]
24. The symbolic language of human communication, its formation and function, eludes every comparison and every analogy which could lead us to a causal hermeneutic of communication: "modern linguists dwell on the fact that the symbolic language of human beings is of an utterly different order from the various (auditory, tactile, visual and other) means of communication animals employ."[16] The absolute impossibility of their analogical correlation is part of the logical place of *discontinuity* in the evolution from the encephalic function of animals to the spiritual powers of human beings.
25. Similarly, we cannot correlate analogically or locate many spiritual human functions, such as: selective memory, active recalling of recollections, judgment concerning the accuracy of the recollections which have been recalled,

voluntary decision-making, the choice of the words which will express our thoughts with precision – and especially every function of creative inspiration, recognition of the otherness of creative inspiration, existential self-consciousness and recognition of subjective identity.

26. The impossibility of finding where the above spiritual abilities (and many other similar ones) are situated means: their appearance presupposes the coordination of many partial encephalic functions, but a coordination which is never securely rooted in a particular place. The result is the absolute indeterminacy of the location of the encephalic point of departure of these abilities.[17]
27. Given that locating an encephalic starting point of specifically human spiritual capacities is absolutely impossible, the theory of evolution transposes this causal location to the genetic blueprints of the human brain. The transposition is made while admitting the complete absence of the least indications which can suggest a probable validity.[18] Thus the strength of the deductive logical method is the only argument adduced: Since every biological function is written into the genetic code, the spiritual functions of human beings cannot rationally constitute an exception.
28. But this deductive syllogism takes the common causal principle of biological and spiritual functions as given, and therefore their evolutionary *continuity*, when intending to demonstrate the absence of *discontinuity*. It is a typical example of the logical fallacy of circularity.
29. Moreover, when science employs deductive logic, it attributes apodictic validity not only to the formal correctness of its reasoning. The hermeneutic by-products of a general hermeneutic principle, whose validity is subject to control, verify or falsify its apodictic strength. Modern science would have remained tied to the dogmatism of medieval intellectualism if it had insisted merely on formally correct productive syllogisms without subjecting

them to the *falsification* of the general propositions by means of controlling the validity of their byproducts.

30. Linear logic (inductive and deductive) cannot provide an autonomous hermeneutic valuation in science. Its hermeneutic force presupposes valid data that can be traced back evidentially. For this reason the hermeneutic probabilities of the theory of evolution are orientations for research, not apodictic propositions.
31. The theory of evolution probabilizes the conditions for the insertion of spiritual capacities into the genetic code of humankind: Evolving the needs to adapt to group symbiosis, needs which serve the instinct of self-preservation, should have imposed it. This specific probability focuses its hermeneutic logic on a single methodological approach based on mechanistic determinism. It echoes the logic of a one-way tracing back of psychological events to the autonomous working of an instinct – a logic which, at least in post-Freudian epistemology, cannot form adequate hermeneutic propositions.
32. The one-way mechanistic tracing back of psychological events to the autonomous working of an instinct is inadequate as a hermeneutic proposition, because it cannot even account for the well-established dualism of impulses, the universal existence of contrary impulses.[19] An impulse on the instinctive level never functions as an autonomous definitive cause of necessities derived from itself. It always functions in concert with some other opposing impulse, always within a complex of corresponding opposing tendencies and necessities. A deterministic logic cannot interpret phenomena which clearly militate against and invalidate the one-way version of how impulses that defend and conserve the human biostructure work: the phenomenon, for example, of self-sacrifice, of denial of the will, of self-destructive feelings, of suicide – or the revealing case of anorexic in-

fants "that steer themselves of their own accord towards death" proving that their "soul" is determinative of their existence, and incomparably more powerful than the instinct of self-preservation.[20]

33. The probabilities of continuous evolution from the brain functions of animals to the spiritual capabilities of human beings presuppose an exemplary space for possible correlations which becomes zero when the fact of human *freedom* requires a causal explanation. And when with the term "freedom" we do not refer only to the power of making choices, but primarily to the power of human existence to define itself and its practice: the power of the human person "to be that which it is not and not to be that which it is."[21]
34. Probabilities could perhaps be posited, or at least tentative indications of correlation or analogy with some abilities of animals for any other spiritual power of the human person. Freedom especially, the human power of active otherness, reveals that the void or evolutionary discontinuity between animals and human beings is unbridgeable. There is an active otherness of reason, of creativity, of imaginative conception, of social action, of erotic relationship, of moral behavior. "[I]t is difficult at the present time to conceive of any way in which the physiology of the central nervous system, despite the progress it has made with the aid of cybernetics, will ever be able to bridge the abyss which separates the storing, the elaboration and circulation of information in a hyper-complex system from the realities of desire, of effect, of creation."[22]
35. By setting boundaries to natural science, philosophy separates the logical space of the theory of evolution from its claim to interpret the question concerning the meaning of existence and of the world, a claim which destroys its logical space.

Thesis 1

The Postmodern Challenge: A Metaphysical Extension Of Physics

1. "Apophatic" language and "unorthodox" methodology

According to the criteria of modernity, the difference between physics and metaphysics is not confined simply to the non-coincidence of subject matter. It is also located in *language* and *method.*

The language of physics uses constant signifiers, which refer to empirically verifiable facts. The meaningful assembly of signifiers as a proposition obeys the laws of logical syntax. The syntax is logical when the proposition pictures a possible situation in empirical space. Thus the language of physics represents the logical form of reality.

By contrast, the language of metaphysics uses signifiers which have no pictorial-representational relationship with sensory reality – such as: the infinite, the timeless, the non-spatial, the immaterial, the uncreated, the causeless, the soul, God. The linguistic logic of the propositions of metaphysics may be formally correct, that is to say, it may have a syntactic order that conveys meaning, an order which permits comprehension. But it does not refer to places accessible to empirical representation.

There is an analogous difference in method. Every scientific method in physics is based on presuppositions concerning the empirical verification of theoretical propositions which are stable and subject to repetition. The validity of the method is judged by how it works. And it works by safeguarding the two-way relationship between theoretical propositions and observable facts.

By contrast, metaphysics is scarcely governed by stable methodological presuppositions if at all. The semantic clarifications of a metaphysical proposition become accessible and acceptable by means of perceptual approaches which are not subject to methodological constants: by means of intuition, discernment, discrimination, insight, patterns of personal experience, confidence in the author of the proposition, etc.

It is well known that physics, under the general imposition of the modern "paradigm," began to doubt in practice the modern assumptions of scientific language and method. I define as "post-Newtonian" the physics which was led by the demands of research to use an "apophatic" language for the formulation of scientific conclusions, with an "unorthodox" version of the hermeneutic methods to formulate these conclusions.

Let us at the outset explore the meaning which I attribute to the terms "apophatic" and "unorthodox:"

I describe as "apophatic" that linguistic semantics and attitude to cognition which refuses to exhaust the content of knowledge in its formulation, which refuses to exhaust the reality of the things signified in the logic of the signifiers. It consequently refuses to verify knowledge merely by controlling the correct representational logic of the signifiers.

Independently of the etymological derivation and the semantic uses at various times of the term,[1] "apophaticism" is used here to indicate the presumed distinction between signifiers and things signified (a distinction not obvious in modernity). The semantic formulation has a relative, indicative and referential character. It suggests reality, but does not necessarily represent it in a definitive and exhaustive manner. It refers to *relationship* with reality, presuming the dynamic indeterminacy of the relationship, an indeterminacy which relativizes the stable interpretation of observation and the representational consistency of the formulation of the conclusions.

When of course the empirical approach to reality, with experiential consistency, is not directly possible (e.g. in the case of subatomic space or of unifying theories), then the semantics of the hermeneutic propositions are relativized further: There is the additional factor of the impossibility of separating the method from the means of the indirect approach to the things signified.

At any rate, in all cases, the apophatic interpretation of the signifiers has nothing to do with irrationality, with mysticism, or with any other individualistic, rather than social, epistemological claim.

In immediate correlation with this interpretation of apophaticism, I describe as "unorthodox" every epistemological method which refuses to function and be imposed as a methodologically correct and cognitively valid code. Without sacrificing methodological consistency, I do not make an absolute of it, nor in consequence do I tie it to a single methodological constant. "Unorthodox" methodology functions as a methodical approach to knowledge, free from subjection to the codification of the methodicity. Thus any known or new epistemological-scientific method can be considered "unorthodox" when it does not claim exclusive rights to methodological correctness.

The demands of research have led post-Newtonian physics to the use of apophatic language and unorthodox research methods.

By post-Newtonian physics I mean the understanding of physical reality which begins to take shape with the appearance of Max Planck's quantum theory of energy (1900), Albert Einstein's special theory of relativity (1905), Niels Bohr's establishment of quantum mechanics (1913), the general theory of relativity (1916), Louis de Broglie's theory of wave-particle duality (1924), Werner Heisenberg's uncertainty principle (1925), Erwin Schrödinger's matter-wave hypothesis of quantum mechanics (1926), the probabilistic understanding of the behavior of matter introduced by Max Born (1928), P.M. Dirac's theory of anti-matter (1930), Richard Feynman's creation of quantum electrodynamics (1950), etc.

This innovative research in physics (which certainly is not exhausted by the above names) overturned a number of the fundamental certainties of modern or Newtonian physics. We could say – in an over-schematic way – that Newtonian physics pictured the world as a mechanically organized whole consisting of given entities correlating to and influencing each other, with the same strict causality and determinism regardless of their number and size. By extending the time-space constants, the causality and regularity which the physical phenomena of our everyday macroscopic experience manifest, modern physics maintained that it could attach precise laws to every phenomenon, that it could attribute full and universal validity to mechanistic causality.

By contrast, physics today gives us a picture of matter, and consequently of the world, as a totality of dynamically uncertain active relations. "There are no 'wheels and gears' in this analysis of Nature," Feynman concludes epigrammatically. "Nature permits us to calculate only probabilities [...] the way we have to describe Nature is generally incomprehensible to us," that is, to common (mechanistic) logic.[2]

Alastair Rae adds: "The idea of the physical universe as an assemblage of interacting but independently existing microscopic particles is not only deeply rooted in our thinking, but is considered by some to be essential to a complete physical theory. A model of the physical world that attributes all reality to the changes, while stating that it is impossible to make a consistent description of what is changing, is difficult to accept."[3]

But if it is impossible to make a consistent description of the dynamic of changes that give rise to physical reality, it is also impossible to use an established codified methodology of consistent description. Just as it is also impossible to use a language which echoes the logic of stable definitions and definite determinations.

The utilitarian communicative intentionality of common language necessarily presupposes a definite rationality which does not coincide with the uncertainty of natural becoming. For this reason we have also seen Feynman emphasizing that the way we have of describing nature is unintelligible to common logic.

Two specific aspects or facets may be noted – briefly and succinctly – of how the dynamic of natural becoming does not comply with a definite language and method.

1. The first refers to the given uncertainty of physical phenomena on a microscopic scale. In the case of an elementary particle, the more accurately we define its *position*, the less accurately we can measure its *speed*, and vice versa. Heisenberg managed to capture this uncertainty in a fundamental "principle": he showed that if we multiply the uncertainty in the position of the particle by the uncertainty in its velocity (speed by mass) we have a figure which can never be smaller than a certain quantity, which is known as Planck's constant – constant h.[4]

In this case, every way of defining the *position* (every consistent procedure of measurement and definition) necessarily relativizes every consistent way of defining the *speed*, and vice versa. The dynamic changeables, *position* and *speed* can only be defined "functionally," that is to say, only in the context of their combination, which is presupposed by every partial procedure of measurement.

The linguistic consequence of the above is that the signifier "position" does not refer to a signified reality which is clearly distinguished (defined and observable) by its "speed." Both signifiers refer to a single reality always of a relative combination of position and speed.

Indeterminacy often also follows the influence on each other of particles: It has been shown that "separated particles influence each other even when there is no known interaction between them."[5] The reliability of method and language is again undermined in a significant way: We affirm influence on each other without any known (observable – determined by method) interaction. The signifier "influence on each other" refers to a non-definable signified, namely, interaction.

Another fact is the uncertainty of distinguishing between *particle* and *wave*: Particles can sometimes behave like waves and waves like particles. In quantum physics we speak of *wave-particle duality* and consequently of *spatial delocalization*.[6] All the electromagnetic forces (all the physical systems with dynamic variables – position, impetus, speed, energy – equivalent to a certain value – h) behave with this dual character, both as waves and as particles, which "gives rise to difficult conceptual problems," since "the concepts of particle and wave are for physics contradictory."[7] Wave-particle duality was originally observed in the case of photons and electrons, but "it appears that all the 'particles' in Nature – quarks, gluons, neutrinos, and so forth [...] – behave in this quantum mechanical way."[8]

Wave-particle duality refers to the "behavior" of elementary units of matter-energy, a behavior that does not conform to the semantics of stable concepts and to the established principles of a single method. The indeterminism of the behavior constitutes a mode of existence, that is, an ontology of the unpredictable, the probable and the possible. On the criteria of modern positivism such an ontology should be described unequivocally as metaphysical. And similarly metaphysical is the synecdochical language of concepts contradictory to physics – on the linguistic level the signifier "wave-particle" functions like the signifier "God-man (*theanthrôpos*)" or

"Mother-virgin (*mêtroparthenos*)."

Unpredictability refers also to the temporal duration or occasion of events, which is not always predeterminable, does not always follow a "forward" direction in time. Every particle has a "latitude" of probability which allows it to move "backwards in time" and this mathematical movement "backwards in time" finds experimental verification as the presence of an anti-particle.[9] The anti-particle of the electron, for example, is defined as a positron – the movement of the electron "backwards in time" lends it a positive charge and thus makes it ontologically different from the electron, which is always negatively charged.[10] Only the photon is at the same time both a particle and an anti-particle, a fact with fertile ontological consequences.

The destabilization of the one-way flow of time and of the definitive ontological identity of any event undermines the constants of "representational" or "re-representational" rationality, the key definitiveness of method and language. The same result is also attained by the refutation of constants which are the coordinates of space – "the non-locality implicit in quantum physics is an inevitable fact of nature."[11] In experimental practice "the 45° photon passing through the HV polarizer does not pass through one channel or the other, but in some way we find very difficult to model it passes through both."[12]

Within the criteria of modern positivism, the relativization and the refutation of the one-way flow of time and the constants of the separability of space – the reversal of before and after and the possibility of "spatial non-localization" – leads to a concept of reality which overturns modern physics, a concept which the positivists would have called metaphysical. They would have applied the same term to the doubting of the ontological constant of elementary particles, to the possibility that we should accept their ontological identification as a pattern of relationships and not as a definitive fact. At least on the linguistic level, signifiers such as "non-locality," the "backward" flow of time, the change of state by which an elementary event receives energy, function in a manner analogous to the metaphysical signifiers of "timeless," "spaceless," "freedom from the biophysical constants of existence."

The indeterminacy of phenomena and the relativity of method and language become even more striking when we turn to biological phenomena: "The vast majority of biological problems still remain outside the capabilities of a purely physical approach."[13] Even if the physicists discover all the fundamental laws of nature, the phenomena of life and consciousness, the way in which these come about will remain unanswerable questions.[14] "For a long time it has been recognized that the living organism cannot be understood, described or analyzed except by means of concepts foreign to physics [...] the living being in general is first of all characterized – logically, phenomenologically and really – by the fact that it establishes a system of partitions within the physical world which is valid only for itself (and, in a series of recessive overlappings, for those "of its kind") and which, since it is only one of an infinite number of possible systems, is wholly arbitrary from the point of view of physics."[15]

Of course, the fact that biological phenomena, to a large extent, remain outside the capabilities of a purely physical approach, does not mean that biology constitutes metaphysics. It means, however, that the boundaries of physics and metaphysics cannot be set where modernity placed them. Just as biology remains non-compliant with physics, without ceasing to constitute an immediate empirical reality, other manifestations of existential fact can similarly be non-compliant with physics but equally accessible to empirical confirmation (even if not subject to representational positivism).

2. The second "aspect" or "facet" of the non-compliance of the dynamic of physical becoming with a definitive lan-

guage and method is the relativity which is imposed by the influence of the act of observation on the physical phenomena that are observed – the need to include the observer (his instruments and his method) in the results.

"A description of the phenomena independently of the method and the means of the observation is impossible."[16] Which means that the primary claim of modern science to "objectivity" (objective conclusion, objective confirmation, and finally objective knowledge) is proved in practice to be unattainable. A human being cannot be a neutral observer of nature, as Newtonian mechanics wished it to be. The attaining of a distance of the observer from the things observed, a distance which permits the observer to objectivize the things observed and to describe them completely independently of his or her own contribution as an observer, is unachievable.

Already the theory of relativity had proved that the result of macroscopic observation is always connected with the position and motion of the observer. Within the context of quantum physics it became evident that the result of the observation of the microcosm is connected also with the instruments, and also with the method of observation and description: "[T]he nature of the model required to describe a system depends on the nature of the apparatus it is interacting with: light is a wave when passing through a pair of slits, but it is a stream of photons when it strikes a detector or a photographic film."[17]

Consequently our perception of reality can change in accordance with our instruments or our method of observation. Observed reality can be transformed by the fact of observing it: "Measurement chooses one or more of the possible states which exist originally within a system, and after the measurement the system remains not in its original state but in that which the measurement has chosen."[18]

Every measurement, or whatever other form of invention which observation takes, constitutes a *relationship* between the observer and the things observed: a relationship consisting of the observer's subjective choices and presuppositions, and also of the difference of correspondences or applications between the things observed and the assumptions of the observation. "Quantum theory tells us that nothing can be measured or observed without disturbing it, so that the role of the observer is crucial in understanding and physical process. So crucial in fact that some people have been led to believe that it is the observer's mind that is the only reality – that everything else, including the whole physical universe, is an illusion."[19]

This last interpretation reflects modernity's desire for a positive "objectivization" of reality or illusion. With a more consistent reliance, however, on the assumptions of quantum physics, it would be more fruitful to accept the logos, or rational character, of the relationship between observer and things observed as the only reality, the fact of the meeting between two balanced indeterminate (methodologically and linguistically) logoi of "personal" otherness: between the logos (of the mind, will, judgment, imagination) of the observer and the logos of a dynamic creative otherness which is observable and active in nature.

Certainly our need to communicate imposes the objectivization of the signifiers of the dialogue between humanity and nature. The objectivization, however, is clearly conventional. Even the signifiers of fundamental physical units reflect a greater degree of reality when they are not strictly defined. Mass, speed, time differ when they are observed within the contexts of different systems of reference. They reflect the reality of the system of reference, not that of constant coordinates for every scientific research project. As constant concepts they refer to a common semantic sense for every scientific research project, but in every scientific research project the things signified are differentiated according to the system of reference.

Consequently only relations formed within the context of various systems of reference have the character of reality: Relations between observable facts leading to the system of reference and to a connection with the method and the means of observation. The dynamic of these real relations corresponds to the uncertainty of their signification and the relativity of the signifiers of the signification.

We said above that the theory of relativity had already demonstrated, at least for the facts of time and space, that they do not constitute a fixed background against which various events occur: "In the theory of relativity there is no unique absolute time, but instead each individual has his own personal measure of time that depends on where he is and how he is moving."[20]

We could say that quantum mechanics has proved very clearly the "relative" character of relativity itself. When we speak of *relations* in quantum mechanics, we do not refer to predictable correlations, nor to a definitive referentiality which creates stable mutual coordinations. When we speak of relations in quantum mechanics, we refer to a *mode* of correlation – referentiality – coordination which has the character of the unpredictable, of the probable, of the possible, and which could be compared only with the dynamic freedom of interpersonal human relations. Quantum mechanics has come to assert "within the very nature of things" a probabilistic character which "is not a result of the imperfection of our instruments of measurement or a lack of sufficient accuracy in calculation,"[21] but constitutes the given *mode* of physical reality. It is a mode which destroys every mechanistic determinism (causality and predictability), demonstrating that the dynamic indeterminacy of *relations* is not symptomatic of irrational chance, but is the rational structural and cohesive factor underlying all physical becoming, the *a priori* principle "of the amazing fact of the stability of the structures of the microcosm."[22]

Scientific observation intervenes in this dynamic indeterminacy of *relations* as a similarly dynamic *participation* in the relations. A participation which itself also constitutes a fact of relationship and influences the relations amongst which it intervenes. The rational character (*logos*) of the observer encounters the rational character (*logos*) of the observed, with the result that an unpredictable *dialogue* (*dia-logos*) is created which is always something different from two parallel and predictable monologues.

The scientific character of the intervention of the observer or "encounter" between the observer and the observed lies in the consequently deliberate exclusion of any possibility that the "monologue" of the observer should be imposed on the observation – a subjective arbitrariness or delusion, a one-sided methodological bias, a subjection of the things observed to the key presuppositions of the observation. We must be aware of *where* and *how* we intervene: that we intervene in a dynamic of relations and within the mode of the relation; we do not decipher objective logical constants or key operations of natural laws in a one-sided way. If we objectivize one of the factors of the dynamic of relations, the others elude us or are minimized in our cognitive signification. To return to the measurement of position and speed, "the more accurately you try to measure the position of the particle, the less accurately you can measure its speed, and vice versa [...]. In this theory particles no longer had separate, well-defined positions and velocities that could not be observed. Instead, they had a quantum state, which was a combination of position and velocity."[23]

The observation shapes its object; the object is constituted only as something observed in accordance with the form of the experimental intervention of the observer. It is not an object in relation to the subject, but is the relationship itself – a kind of free response of the thing observed to the observation. In this context one may venture the formulation, that the natural object comes to have "subjective" properties: Not the freedom of the subject's existential self-definition, but the indeterminacy of a personal *logos* in activity. And the revealing dynamic of the personal *logos* is not exhausted in a fixed definition of signifiers, nor is it subordinated to the key presuppositions of a method. For this dynamic to become known, a language and method is required which will refer to the fact of the *relation* as an integral whole without subordinating it to objectivizing generalizations.

The postmodern approach to the way natural becoming is constituted and functions requires us to withdraw from the simply representational or image-forming capacity of our mind, from the constants of an "ontic" understanding of the existent and the real. This withdrawal serves the *apophatic* use of language in the formulation of the conclusions of modern physics. That is why the expression of physical science often seems to border on poetic imagery (poetic freedom in using antithetical meanings or abusing signifiers to manifest the otherness and universality of the rational character of the relation).

We read, for example, about particles which although situated at enormous distances from each other, make up a unified whole within a non-localized totality. That the quanta of energy do not exist in space, but create space. We read about "virtual particles" which can never be traced directly but their existence has measurable effects on other particles. About the possibility of using "imaginary time" in scientific research, with the aim of bringing quantum theory into models for the "anomaly" of space-time. Or even about the completely different form of particles which play a part in micro-events and are verified by research to be one and the same particle in different states. Or we are informed by modern theories of "superstrings" that the structural entities of physics are nooses which create the different forms of particles as they dangle in a "space" of ten dimensions.

In reality, the analog of such language is found only in poetic imagery. It allows us to speak of non-localized distance, of a nonexistence that exists and is measured as an effect, of a wave which is not a wave but a particle, of a particle which is not a particle but a wave, of the many which are one, of the one which is many.

One can use many analogous examples of images that fill out the representational insufficiency in contemporary physics: one may recall the "curved" nature of space-time, which becomes infinite in the center of "black holes," just as it was infinite at the moment of the Big Bang. Or the stopping of time when we transcend the "event horizon" which surrounds a black hole. Or the view that fundamental time is "imaginary," while the time which we perceive and verify is simply a product of our macroscopic experience. Or one may recall the tachyons which ever elude experimental research, for the more their energy weakens the more quickly they move, reversing the relationship of cause and effect.

Nor can we claim that our weakness for a representational understanding of the reality of the smallest and greatest dimensions is satisfied by the "clarity" of the language of mathematical forms and symbols. For mathematicians' language has never sought a representational function for the explanation of entities; it is a language of relations. Even in the definition of quantities, in the physics of the smallest and greatest spaces, the language of mathematics transcends the so called "human system"[24] (the boundaries of human perceptive capacities). The attribution of objective subsistence to mathematical concepts, which has so occupied philosophy (from Plato and Descartes to Kurt Gödel) as also the identification of truth with demonstrability, are issues which are not raised within the context of contemporary mathematical science. The needs of physics created and continue to create new branches of mathematics, in which mathematical proofs are valid but relative: dependent on the axiomatic context of the theory to which they are subject.

The mathematical language of a proposition in contemporary physics is indicative and demonstrative, rather than representational. For this reason it can also demonstrate by itself the presuppositions of relations which are not confirmed by observation, or are indicated by equations "the content of which we do not entirely understand."[25] Frequently the equations in a contemporary physics paper function rather like the score of a symphony: We "read" and perceive the melodies but no melody is ever represented formally or schematically.

Modern physics was identified (and with the very broad popularization of positivism continues to be identified) with "objective" science *par excellence*: It was linked with the certainty of stable localizations – measurements – experimental repetitions, and this certainty was based on key methodologies and on a language signifying definitive definitions. Thus on the criteria of the positivistic ideology of modernity, the *unorthodox* methodology and *apophatic* language of post-Newtonian science seems to constitute a preliminary aspect of a metaphysical extension of physics.

2. The relativity of space and time

On the criteria of modern positivism, the new interpretation of space and time within the context of contemporary research could be described as a metaphysical extension of physics. The positivistic separation of physics and metaphysics appears to be undermined by the relativization of space and time, the verification of the nonexistence of absolute or objective space and time. Our view of the fact of existence is radically transformed if space and time are not constants which "contain" and "measure" the fact of existence but rather it is the fact of existence which "measures" or defines the relations which constitute it by the rules of space and time.

Even Newtonian physics could call into doubt at least the Aristotelian understanding of space as the "motionless boundary" which "contains" existent things, that is, which objectivizes the phenomena in stable positions, distances and sizes. "Place," said Aristotle, "is the innermost motionless boundary of what contains it, like a non-portable vessel."[26] Newtonian physics asserted that this "motionless boundary" does not exist, since a body's absolute state of tranquility does not exist, which would have been able, as a system of reference, to define constants of position and speed.

Newtonian theory, however, did not take this assertion through to its conclusion: It resorted to the hypothesis that an indeterminate substance must exist, the "ether," which fills the three-dimensional cosmic space, and that the absolute positions and stable laws of motion within space are defined in relation to motionless ether. Questions about where the boundaries of the ether extended and what existed beyond those boundaries were not raised.

The consequences of the nonexistence of absolute states of stillness were spelled out by the theory of relativity: Spatial location is always relative, always connected with changeable systems of reference, always presupposing taking the position and movement of the observer into account. Nobody can define whether two facts at different moments in time coincided at the same point in space or not. "It is not possible to step twice into the same river," said Heraclitus,[27] and a modern paradigmatic image is the ping-pong ball that bounces on the same spot in the carriage of a moving train. For someone in the carriage the ball bounces in a defined spatial position. For someone outside the train or in a train moving in the opposite direction, the same ball bounces in completely different positions in relation to different coordinates.[28]

For the theory of relativity, space is an interconnected set of active relations – it is continuously destroyed as an objective reality by the very dynamic of the relations. And the destruction of objective space also "involves" the way in which we view the existence of absolute or objective time. This "involvement" may be represented by the example of the different chronological measurements of the emission-reflection-return of a pulse of light with regard to the location in space of the same object measured by different moving instruments. In experimental practice, pulses of light are sent out by the instruments, are reflected by the same object, and return to the instruments, which, however, give different results of measurement (duration of time and length of passage) for the same location – in spite of the measurements being carried out by the same method. From another perspective the measurement of distance and duration, of time and space, although a constant, only demonstrates the speed of light.[29]

The example portrays, in a necessarily elliptical fashion, an experimental certainty: We cannot use the measurements of distance and time as constants for the determination of the speed of light. We can, however, use the speed of light as a constant measurement for the determination of distance and time. Distance and time are dimensions that change in accordance with our relative movement. Conversely, an indisputable constancy is only possessed by the speed of light. Up to the present, no experimental fact has cast any doubt on this conclusion.

Formulating it differently, we could say that light does not move within an objective space, nor can its speed be measured by some temporal constant. Since the transmission of light is our only available means to establish the position and the moment in time of real physical facts, the speed of this transmission is the only stable measure of the location of objects in space and time – it is the transmission of light which creates space and time. We define the position and the time of light's emission or reflection only by the constant of its speed, which remains unchanged in whatever way we move to shift our terrestrial perspective. Only by using the speed of light as a measure can we determine the distance which separates us from the objects that emit or reflect light, and also the moment in time of the emission or reflection in relation to ourselves.

But a uniform measure is also correlative to something measured that is of the same kind. (Measurement is possible only when the measure is appropriate to the object measured, and for this reason, according to the Aristotelian as well as the Newtonian view, a tape measures only distance and a clock measures only duration.) As a uniform standard of measurement, the speed of light is correlative to a uniform and homogenous meaning of space and time: in the unitary reality of *space-time*, accessible only through the study of the reality of light.

We conceive of space-time as four-dimensional. It is constituted by the three dimensions of space plus a fourth dimension of time. As in three-dimensional space, so the representational transcription of the movement of bodies in four-dimensional space-time can give us geometry. But in the case of space-time, not a Euclidean geometry.

Observation confirms that the orbits of bodies within the universe follow curved paths. Newtonian physics attributed the elliptical orbits of the heavenly bodies to the attractive force of gravity, which always depends on the mass and distance of bodies. But for attractive force to change automatically in accordance with distance, gravitational influences must be transmitted with infinite speed. The theory of relativity showed that such a speed is impossible, and the elliptical orbits of the heavenly bodies are the result of the curvature of space-time. According to the general theory of relativity, gravity is not a force, but something resembling the property of a field, whose geometry is formed by the distribution of mass-energy: the transmission of light – the only means and measure of positioning within space-time – follows the curvatures of the gravitational field and creates a geometry of curved space. Both the movements of bodies with mass, and the transmission of light which has no mass (although it "informs" mass and movement – renders it an eidetic fact) follow curved paths.

We define a straight line as the shortest distance between two points. The shortest distance between two points, however, differs in non-Euclidean geometry from Euclidean. Which geometry makes the orbits of the heavenly bodies in the universe and light appear curved? Clearly the Euclidean understanding of the space of our terrestrial experience. The shortest transit, even within four-dimensional space-time, is straight, but we perceive the straight transit within space-time as a curve of three-dimensional space because of the transmission of light.

In the representational transcription of the movement of the heavenly bodies we say that "the orbit coincides with the shortest line. And the shortest line in a modified (non-Euclidean) geometry is not a straight line. The way in which the shortest lines are defined in a given (non-Euclidean) geometry is a purely mathematical problem which had been studied by mathematicians long before Einstein."[30]

Could we then draw the conclusion that the orbits of the heavenly bodies and the transmission of light within the universe only *appear* curved and are not *really* curved? But since the means and the measure of observation is only the transmission of light, *appearance* cannot be differentiated from *reality*. The propositions: light is bent in a curve, the orbits of the heavenly bodies are curved, space-time obeys a curved geometry, are propositions which refer to a unified and homogeneous "eidetic" interpretation of reality.

It is our observations and measurements which assure us that the transmission of light is curved and especially in conjunction with the presence of matter. Matter exercises a gravitational influence on light. When we speak of "matter" we are referring to the combination of mass and energy. When light comes near a body (a fact of mass-energy) we can verify that it is slowed down in its transmission. In relation to which constant of time is it slowed down? Only in relation to the frequency of its transmission: the number of light waves which pass a given point per second per unit of measurement used to establish frequency.[31]

The passage of light becomes curved when the transmission frequency of light is reduced. And the frequency is reduced when the light approaches matter, since matter exercises a gravitational influence on light. Matter causes the curvature of the means by which we locate it, which is the transmission of light, and consequently also of the coordinates of its location: of space and time – the curvature of space-time. There is no space and time without the transmission of light which "informs" – makes mass and movement an "eidetic" fact. The presence of light alone does not create space and time.[32] The transmission of light is presupposed, curved by the gravitational pull of matter, so that space and time are constituted to determine the curvature of every movement and orbit in the universe.

Space and time are revealed, within the context of contemporary physics, as combinations of the presence of matter alone – as products (quantities) of the measurement of the transmission of light's frequency, a frequency which is influenced by the gravitational force of the mass-energy of material bodies.

If space and time are combinations and products of the presence of matter, then that which exists materially is not "within" space and time. Space and time do not "contain" what exists, but are consequences of the materiality of what exists (of mass-energy and the gravitational forces which it exercises).

This means that any question relating to the fact of existence in itself ("being *qua* being" – the beingness of being, the existence of that which exists), and consequently also to the concept of the cause of existence – any question to do with ontology or metaphysics – cannot be posed with presuppositions and associations of space and time. The question of what exists with regard to its property that it actually exists (before the inclusion of materiality in the assertion of its existence) excludes any connotation of space and time in the fact of existence.

This is a logical consequence which seems completely abstract. It has, however, a vital significance for clarifying the field of research. Perhaps the inclusion of materiality in the assertion of existence is obligatory, or perhaps not. If both possibilities are open to research, we cannot restrict such research to the presuppositions of only one possibility: we cannot seek to clarify the fact of existence, its meaning and its cause, with presuppositions of ontological determination, that is, with the representational logic of spatial and temporal localizations. Even the conceptual expansion of space and time to infinity (the use of the concepts "unlimitedness," "infinity," "eternity") must be excluded from ontology in the proper sense, because it ties us to the bounds of physics (especially Newtonian physics). Only signifiers of "existence" derived from the coordinates of space and time are "legitimized" within the context of the ontological problem. And this "legitimization" is supported by the conclusions of contemporary physics.

But can we present a convincing argument for existence that does not entail materiality without our resorting to empirically untestable abstract ideas, arbitrary subjective experiences, or convinctions accessible only through the emotions?

The question can be extended in various directions. In the context of space and time we can only study existence as a fact in relation to the space-time coordinates of the location of materiality.

The observations and studies of Edwin Hubble have led to the more or less unanimous acceptance of a beginning of the universe in time. It has been asserted that the universe is constantly expanding, that the galaxies are moving further apart from each other with speeds which in some case are approaching that of light. The distancing of the galaxies from each other is not the result of any cosmic forces, but of a given initial impulse. The interpretation of this origin refers to an initial Big Bang, the explosion of the universe's matter-energy in its primary super-dense state. Recently this interpretation has been decisively strengthened by the discovery of a "residual radiation" which cannot otherwise be explained.

We are also led to the acceptance of a Big Bang, that is, of a beginning in time of the universe, by the mathematical location of events in space-time posited by Einstein's General Theory of Relativity. With Einstein's equations "we find that in all past events of space-time the existence of a field in which the density of matter and the curvature of geometry become infinite is predicted. It is usually expressed by saying that the equations predict a singularity of space-time in which density and curvature become infinite. This singularity describes the Big Bang that created the universe. Moreover, and indeed more importantly, the theory does not let us ask what existed or what happened *before* the Big Bang. Because in space-time, which from its formation includes all events in space and time, there is nothing before that unique event. We can say that nothing happened and nothing existed before the Big Bang, because before it there was neither space nor time, and consequently there was no 'before'."[33]

The theory excludes any inquiry into the *before* of the Big Bang, just as it excludes any inquiry into *where* it took place. Space has a beginning like time: the beginning of space is the point of infinite density and curvature, the moment of the Big Bang. Beyond this point there is no space, just as there is none beyond the bounds of the universe. The expanding universe constitutes space (and time) and outside this expansion there is no space (or time).

The exclusion of any inquiry into the "before" and the "where" of the beginning of the universe is imposed by the assertions of physics and imposes a purely metaphysical concept: the concept of an obligatory exit from the succession of before and after, and also from every dimensional location. Such a concept may also entail the exit from the presupposition of the existent, or it may not. Contemporary physics seems to say that it does not.

Apparently it does not, marking certain *a priori* constants at the outset which we must regard as facts created at the "zero" moment of the Big Bang and without which the Big Bang would have resulted not in the creation of the universe but rather in the complete annihilation of the hyper-dense primeval elements which exploded.

When we speak of *a priori* or "fundamental" natural constants we refer to "those parameters which cannot be calculated theoretically but must be taken as primeval empirical facts [...]. The masses of proton and electron, the electronic charge and Planck's constant are fundamental constants. For the time being nobody knows how they can be calculated theoretically. All the physical masses, the constants yoking together the fundamental fields and the speed of light belong to the same category."[34] The arithmetical values of these parameters are given on the basis of the arbitrary macroscopic system of units which we have chosen; we ascribe conventional values with a view to defining comparative correlations with the other physical parameters.

From the indeterminate and "arbitrary" – for us – numerical value, however, which the fundamental physical constants had in the timeless moment of the Big Bang, the existence of the universe became possible. The least differentiation between them would have destroyed the possibility of material existence. Contemporary physics proves this through the conventional but apodictic means of comparative relational measurements.

When we speak of "given" values, of the fundamental physical constants in the timeless moment of the Big Bang, we refer to a "selection" which is inherent in the fact of the Big Bang and determines it. We can in an arbitrary way (and not with the help of physics) interpret this "selection" as a product of "chance," a result of "an improbable throw of the dice"[35] which brought at its first and only attempt the appropriate conjunctions from within an infinity of possibilities. But even in this case without a "logical space" the inherent "selection" which determines the event of the Big Bang, whether fortuitous or not, refers us to a given "before" which has no temporal antecedent, although it *exists* as a predetermination (fortuitous or intentional) of the specific fact.

Physics cannot inquire into the effective cause of the Big Bang. Its calculations become infinite at the precise point and moment of the Big Bang. Nevertheless physics marks out the (fortuitous or intentional) presuppositions which defined the Big Bang as an event responsible for establishing the universe as we know it today. This "marking out" constitutes an "involuntary" extension of the physical "boundary" of the confirming conclusion: a metaphysical extension of physics.

Indeed, the "arbitrary" but presuppositionary values of the physical constants of the universe which guarantee its existence "are the 'metaphysical' facts of physics."[36] Just as it is also a metaphysical fact of physics that the event of the Big Bang happened – although there is no "exemplary space" of possibilities from which the Big Bang can emerge as a probability. It is a metaphysical given of physics that time and space have a specific beginning in conditions negating them,[37] "within" their non-temporality and non-locality, that is, in a metaphysical or pre-physical context. This context is meta-physical or pre-physical, because it is confirmable by physics (and therefore "real") and at the same time excludes the questions posed by physics.

And most importantly: Both the specifications (fortuitous or intentional) of the Big Bang as a founding event of the universe, and the non-local and non-temporal coordinates of the beginning of space and time are determined and therefore "existential" facts, principles of existential uniqueness, without entailing materiality in the definition of their existence.

The exit from the succession of before and after, as well as from any dimensional location, may or may not be an exit also from the presuppositions of the existent. Contemporary physics appears to say no, in the cases just mentioned, and also in the behavior of the elemental particles of matter-energy.

"The laws of science do not distinguish between the past and the future."[38] An electron can move "backward in time" and constitute a positron, that is, it can be equally existent both then and when it moves "forwards" in time. And a photon can pass simultaneously through both slits of a polarizer, abolishing the "where" but remaining demonstrably existent.

This freedom from time and space can be measured experimentally because it does not entail the destruction of existence. "The backwards-moving electron when viewed with time moving forwards appears the same as an ordinary electron, except it's attracted to normal electrons – we say it has a 'positive charge.' […]. For this reason it's called a 'positron.' The positron is a sister particle to the electron, and is an example of an 'anti-particle.' This phenomenon is general. Every particle in Nature has an amplitude to move backwards in time, and therefore has an anti-particle. When a particle and its anti-particle collide, they annihilate each other and form other particles. (For positrons and electrons annihilating, it is usually a photon or two.) And what about the photons? Photons look exactly the same in all respects when they travel backwards in time [...] so they are their own anti-particles."[39]

One could object that formulations of the kind set out above transfer into ordinary speech conventional forms of mathematical analysis using the terms "time" and "space," but without a semantic correspondence to what we call time and space in ordinary speech. But even if we accept this objection, it is difficult for us to exclude the reference to physical reality which the transfer to the language of the forms of mathematical analysis requires. The linguistic version of mathematical analysis refers to a specific view or interpretation of physical reality – it attempts to "utter" the reality, as this emerges from within the fixed points of mathematical symbolism – just as our everyday language refers to another perspective or interpretation of physical reality – from within *fixed points* which are sensory and accessible to the common macroscopic perception.

The fact is that both of these uses of linguistic semantics – the language of everyday communication and the translation into the language of the forms of mathematical symbolism – claim equally to demonstrate the real and the existent. Of course our everyday language is the more useful and corresponds in a more immediate way to the needs of practical communication within the common macroscopic perception of the real. But there are no criteria that make it more consistent with the demonstration of reality than the linguistic version of mathematical symbolics. On the contrary, the linguistic version of mathematical symbolics was developed in order to compensate for the inadequacy of our everyday language in describing reality in the smallest and the greatest dimensions.

Significantly, contemporary physics provides us with a language which manifests the relativity of time and space or even of the freedom from time and space of what exists, a language which until now had been appropriated exclusively by metaphysics. Expressed in our everyday language of macroscopic localization, the freedom from space and time of some manifestations of what exists still has metaphysical implications. Formulated, however, with the linguistic semantics of natural science, this very freedom refers to signified objects of physical reality.

The difference between the two linguistic codes is a difference of provenance (from conventional forms of macroscopic significations or conventional forms of mathematical process) and also a difference of associations. In spite of these differences, however, the signified referred to is the same and remains common – the signified fact is not differentiated by difference of provenance or the associations conveyed by the two linguistic codes.

And, more importantly, there exists a common presupposition of cognitive approach to the signified, which unites the two linguistic codes, independently of their provenance and of whether they refer to metaphysical associations or mathematical symbols: Both linguistic codes require us equally to transcend the representational or imaging nature of the way we think. As either a metaphysical or natural signified, the freedom from time and space of certain manifestations of existence becomes accessible to us (regardless of the code of linguistic semantics employed) with conceptual capacities other than the representational re-forming of sensory images.

The transcendence of the representational re-forming of sensory images does not necessarily entail an extra-sensory, exclusively intellectual or imaginary, conception of the "real." If time and space are functions of matter and if the existential fact is not necessarily bound by the limitations of time and space, if the existential fact does not have to have material connotations, the consequences are vital for ontology or metaphysics. The error or inadequacy, however, of philosophical metaphysics when investigating this eventuality was always to draw intellectual conclusions from phenomenologocial (macroscopic) starting points of intellectual representations. The error was to rely on philosophical metaphysics for conceptual forms detached from experience, with their simultaneous formal-syllogistic semantic extension – chiefly through the intellectual elevation of natural representations to the level of the conceptual absolute.

Contemporary metaphysical extensions of physics, on the other hand, do not seek to prove the nonexistence of absolute or objective time and space – the freedom of certain manifestations of the existent from time and space – by abstract syllogistic inferences, nor do they make it an autonomous mental concept. They define it as a *mode* of the existential fact, a mode with an undetermined dynamic, a dynamic not subject to objective constants. The dynamic of the mode is signified with the help of mathematical symbols or even with their translation into a linguistic formulation, without losing the clarity of the pragmatic fact: the meaning of the *mode* is not exhausted by, or tied to, causal constants and representational modeling.

To insist on the dynamic indeterminacy of the *modes* of the existential fact does not halt scientific research or imply agnosticism. On the contrary, through the unlimited possibilities of chiefly mathematical symbolism, the insistence on indeterminacy tends towards an extension of experimental perceptiveness: "qualities" of the behavior of existents are signified – not the recasting of macroscopic representations in autonomous conceptual forms.

Our cognitive recognition of "qualities" of the behavior of existents – in the specific dynamic of the *modes* of the existential fact not subject to objective definition – is analogous to the empirical verification of the qualitative multiformity of human creative activity: We recognize experientially the difference between the poetry of Cavafy and that of Seferis, between the music of Mozart and that of Brahms, between the art of Goya and that of Van Gogh. We can never express this difference in objective definitions and conceptual forms. Yet we recognize it by empirical verification. The notation of musical scores, the syntax and vocabulary of poetry, the material and variations of color in art are certain initial constants, which nevertheless refer to a qualitative multiformity of "behaviors" not subject to objective definitions and conceptual forms. They refer to the qualitative difference of the creative *mode* of the artist.[40]

Correspondingly, the mathematical symbols in contemporary physics or the linguistic formulations derived from them refer to the qualitative difference between creative modes of natural becoming. Mathematical and linguistic signifiers are the initial constants, which nevertheless refer to a qualitative multiformity of "behaviors" indicating only a way of discerning – they are discerned simply as rational qualities – such as the qualitative multiformity of the poetic, artistic or musical act of creation.

A distance determined by the measure of the speed of light and expressed by the arithmetical value of billions of light years; determinations of time with the measure of the microsecond (which is equivalent to a millionth of a second); the mean length of "superstrings," which is 10^{20} times smaller than the size of protons; temperatures in the order of 10^{32} degrees Celsius; the non-local universal linking of elementary particles; their movement *backwards* in time; the simultaneous passage of a photon through two different slits; the ten-dimensional "space" in which the initial movements of the quantum field arise; the temporal reversibility of the laws of gravity, electricity and magnetism, nuclear reaction, etc. – all these are examples of signifiers which do not refer to intelligible magnitudes or to intelligible states, nor do they refer to abstract products of syllogistic inference. They are linguistic or arithmetical modes marking out the signification of signified things inaccessible to representational thought, indications of an existential instantiation not subject to intellectual conception. They refer not to a definite intelligible "what," but to a modal "how" – to the *mode* of the existent rather than to its "ontic" representational meaning.

The possibility within the language of contemporary physics for the freedom from space and time of certain manifestations of the existent, freedom from needing material verification of the existent, from referring the "behaviors" of matter-energy to the qualitative difference of natural becoming's creative *mode* – what in the end does it "prove" in relation to metaphysics?

Absolutely nothing – if by the word "proof" we mean compelling reasons for us to accept a metaphysical interpretation and understanding of what exists. A metaphysical interpretation and understanding cannot be a result of the scientific study of the world. Because it constitutes a different *relationship* with the world.

To give a clear idea of this different *relationship* with the world which the possibility of a metaphysical interpretation and understanding offers, we must return to the example of how we approach a work of art:

The scientific study of a work of art may offer us valuable and exhaustive information about the materials, method and technique of its production. It may offer us the fullest analysis of its themes, of the influences that have shaped it, and of the interpretations which it is capable of receiving. But the scientific study of an art object cannot impose upon us that form of the *relationship* with it which allows us to recognize the principle of a personal otherness, the uniqueness of a creative person. Scientific study can possibly convey the personal otherness of the creative principle which is expressed in the work of art, can possibly refer to it. But it can never make it into a cognitive fact. The knowledge of personal otherness is only an experience of *relation*. It presupposes the cognitive empirical immediacy of the relation.

Two conclusions follow from this paradigmatic assertion:

First, if our approach to the work of art is exhausted in its scientific study and analysis, no intellectual (scientifically supported) necessity can force its transformation into a *personal relationship* which makes reference to the recognition of the existential otherness of the artistic creator. Which means: If we accept the physical reality of the world as exclusively an object of scientific study and analysis, no intellectual (scientifically supported) assertion can oblige us to have a *personal relationship* with the world which makes reference to the metaphysical interpretation and understanding of the world – to the recognition of the personal otherness of a creative principle which is expressed in the artifact of the world.

Secondly, the converse of the above conclusion is also valid. When our relationship with the principle of the artifact is *personal* (experiential immediacy of *relation* and not an intellectual conclusion from syllogistic inferences or ideological preferences), no scientific refutation can cast doubt on the experiential reality and immediacy of this relation.

What are we trying to convey with the term *personal relationship* – what elements can be set down objectively to define a personal relationship with any human or cosmic creative artifact?

In the first place the element of the objectively non-presumed coordination of two principles (of the relative appearances) of personal (existential and creative) otherness. The referentiality of the principle of the personal otherness of the creator encounters (through the meaning of the artifact) a personally unique recognition and acceptance of this principle: I recognize, for example, in the music of Mozart that quality which is expressive of the uniqueness which refers me to the unique, distinct and unrepeatable fact of its existential presence. The subjective *mode* of this recognition is *rational*, because although it guarantees me access to the otherness of the objective *logos*, it also constitutes at the same time a *logos*-disclosure of its own existential uniqueness, since it establishes and reveals a unique and distinct relationship of my own with the music of Mozart. The music of Mozart "being one and the same, is participated as one by many hearers," and is participated as a totality, while at the same time "it is participated by all singly."[41]

The second element determinative of a personal relationship: the freedom for its realization. Freedom is not limited to the choice of realizing the relationship or not. It also presupposes the voluntary letting go of intentionalities which destroy the dynamic of the relationship, and turn the relationship into a one-sided submission, a dependence, a utilitarian use of the objective second term of the relationship. The realization of a *personal* relationship is always a struggle for self-transcendence, a struggle for freedom from egocentric intentionalities which neutralize the second term of the relationship, disparage its uniqueness and distinctness, transform it into an impersonal utilitarian appendage of a one-sided need, demand, desire. Without these presuppositions the dynamic of recognition – the dynamic of the personal encounter with an objective principle of personal otherness – does not function.

A metaphysical interpretation and understanding of the world is neither scientificably attainable nor scientifically excluded. It is another mode of cognitive approach to the world, a transition from the (as much as possible) neutral observation of the world to a personal relationship with the world. It is a product of the freedom of humankind, and therefore interpretation and understanding define its entire *stance* towards the world, its mode of use of the world.

The recognition that the world has meaning (recognition rather than intellectual acceptance) is a cognitive fact, which nevertheless emerges from a certain quality of human relations with the world freed from the demands of exclusively intellectual necessities. The same is true of the recognition of an existential "principle" of this meaning, a personal existential cause, to which the otherness of the *logos*, or the creative mode of natural becoming, refers.

In speaking of quality of relations which let us recognize a personal causal principle of the world, we include within their dynamic the freedom of the human person. No necessity – intellectual, utilitarian or axiological – can violate the dynamics of personal relationship, the readiness or the denial of recognition of the personal otherness of the world's *logos*. It depends exclusively on the freedom of the human person to restrict his or her relationship with the world to the limits of scientific study, of utilitarian exploitation, even of the acceptance of mindless chance – or else to broaden and transform the relationship to an experiential encounter with a personal creative *logos*.

The important contribution of contemporary physics to this problem (which here I call a metaphysical extension of physics) is that it does not *a priori* render inadmissable (it does not prove arbitrary or imaginary – as the positivistists of the modern age would have liked) that relationship with the world, the dynamics of which lead to a recognition of a personal causal principle of the world. On the contrary, the language of contemporary physics, fatally undermining the definitive and defining "objectivity" of scientific assertion, liberates and "validates" other modes of cognitive access to the cosmic fact. Most of all, it reduces the difference of method and language for a cognitive approach either to works of art on the human level or artifacts on the cosmic level.

3. The ontological proposition of the "anthropic principle"

The *anthropic principle* makes its appearance within the context of contemporary physics as a proposition analogous to any general scientific "principle" – such as that of relativity, or uncertainty, or Pauli's exclusion principle.

Every principle of this kind is a general rule which comprises a number of partial scientific assertions and refers to some fundamental presupposition of a cognitive approach to the facts of physical becoming. As a compendious summary of partial assertions, a scientific "principle" is a unifying criterion which facilitates general overviews and functions as a methodological and hermeneutic presupposition for understanding the phenomena.

The "anthropic principle" is a general rule of this kind which comprises a number of partial scientific assertions, chiefly from quantum mechanics, but also from the study of cosmological facts, within the context of contemporary physics. One could summarize the anthropic principle in the epigrammatic statement of one of its main spokesmen, John A. Wheeler: "The universe has to be such as to admit life. It is not only that man is adapted to the universe. The universe is adapted to man."[42]

One's first impression on reading such a statement is that the anthropic principle attributes intentionality and consequently "sense" to the existence of the universe. Therefore it is a proposition that goes beyond the range of scientific assertions and ascends to the realm of metaphysical interpretation. But on studying the development of the anthropic principle, this first impression is blunted, though not entirely eradicated. Certainly the "principle" also includes a hermeneutic proposition which goes beyond the assertions. Yet one might say that the formulation of the proposition is made compelling by the lucidity of the assertions: the scientific assertions refer so closely to interpretation that they render the terms of assertion and interpretation obscure.

Nevertheless, within contemporary cosmology the anthropic principle is not defined as a proposition of a hermeneutic character. Its preeminent character is that of a unifying criterion for the general overview of the cosmic phenomenon, that of a methodological principle for a synthesizing critique of how scientific assertions are understood. Scientists make a distinction, however, most of them proposing a "weak" version of the principle, with a minority in favor of a "strong" version. "Few people would quarrel with the validity or utility of the weak anthropic principle."[43]

The *weak* version may be summarized in the following words: "the universe tends from the beginning in an organic fashion towards the creation of conditions for its self-cognition, that is to say, towards the creation of conditions of rational life." Within this perspective of an innate and verifiable "tendency" of the universe, "life is properly a holistic phenomenon, the existence of which is due to the functioning together of all the natural laws and all the elements of physical reality."[44]

It is evident from this brief summary that the weak anthropic principle presupposes what is fundamentally a teleology of the laws of physics, which may be deduced from the scientific assertion: The formation of the universe is consequent upon intentionality – a presuppositional "natural selection" directs the process of becoming in nature towards that final form in which matter can acquire consciousness of its existence.

A deductive teleology, however, can also function as a starting-point for research: this is the methodological proposition of the weak anthropic principle. The fact that *life exists* constitutes a criterion or guiding orientation for the understanding and interpretation of the functioning of natural laws and the process of becoming in the universe. The existence of life is an "experiential fact" with an almost unlimited informative value for the universe and its laws.

With regard both to the general form of natural laws and to the values of the natural constants which the laws contain, the existence of life imposes serious restrictions. A single unimportant deviation either in the form of the laws or in the values of their constants would destroy the possibility of the existence of life in the universe The possibility is not destroyed, life exists, consequently the fact of its existence is a constant of cognitive theory which constitutes a guiding principle for scientific research.[45]

We investigate and study the laws of nature and the evolving cosmos on the basis of the "experiential" fact of the existence of life. Its concentration on the "natural selection" which guides the process of becoming in nature towards the realization of rational life is a criterion and principle in scientific discourse. The universe is what it is because we human beings are what we are. "If it had been different, we would not be here!"[46]

The *strong* version of the anthropic principle may be summarized in the following statement: Scientific observation does not simply affirm the reality of the cosmos; it constitutes it as an existential fact.

"A quantum theory based on consciousness" says that "the very existence of an external universe, or at least the particular state it is in, is strongly determined by the fact that conscious minds are observing it."[47] But what precisely does such an aphorism mean?

Quantum physics is the fullest and most coherent interpretation today of the behavior of atomic and subatomic systems, that is to say of the very composition of what exists in its microscopic dimension, and the appearance of what exists in its macroscopic dimension. Every appearance of reality becomes possible thanks to the wavelike behavior or wave function of matter in its microscopic dimension. To this behavior is also due the transmission of light: the presupposition of every appearance, every existential assertion in the macrocosm.

The linking of the wavelike behavior of matter with our macroscopic assertions, however, signifies an extension of quantum mechanics into the macrocosm and raises again the so-called "measurement problem" of quantum mechanics: The moment whatever apparatus we are using records the result of a measurement, the wave function which is recorded takes on a specific value dependent upon our method of measurement.[48] All the other probabilities are nullified – the probabilistic character of quantum reality "collapses." That is to say the measurement transforms a potential state into reality. But if quantum theory is of universal application, then even our measuring apparatus is included within the quantum system. Consequently, the reality which an apparatus records will also be subject to probability and without specific meaning, so as to be recorded by a second apparatus which measures the first and which is subject in its turn to the measurement of a third, and so on *ad infinitum*. "At some point in the measurement sequence the quantum description must become invalid, the chain must be broken and it must be possible to say that a physical system is in a particular state."[49]

This does not mean that for quantum physics human consciousness is simply the ultimate measuring apparatus – necessarily but conventionally final in a theoretically infinite sequence of measurements. No. For quantum physics human consciousness is the only possibility of measurement which is not itself subject to the "wave function" of matter, and for this reason constitutes the solution of the measurement problem. Human consciousness rather than the human brain, because the latter is subject to the wave-mechanical behavior of matter.

(Here I may add in parentheses that "[m]any of the perplexing features of the quantum theory can be understood in terms of a curious 'wave-particle' duality, reminiscent of the mind-body duality. According to this idea, a microscopic entity such as an electron or a photon sometimes behaves like a particle and sometimes like a wave; it depends on the sort of experiment chosen. A particle is a totally different animal from a wave; it is a small lump of concentrated stuff, whereas a wave is an amorphous disturbance that can spread out and dissipate. How can anything be both? It all has to do with complementarity again. How can the mind be both thoughts and neural impulses? How can a novel be both a story and a collection of words? Wave-particle duality is another software-hardware dichotomy. The particle aspect is the hardware face of atoms – little balls rattling about. The wave aspect corresponds to the software, or mind, or information, for the quantum wave is not like any other sort of wave anybody has ever encountered. It is not a wave of any substance or physical stuff, but a wave of knowledge or information. It is a wave that tells us what can be known about the atom, not a wave of the atom itself. [...]. The quantum wave is also a wave of probability. It tells you where you can expect the particle to be, and what chance it may have of such-and-such a property, such as rotation or energy. The wave thus encapsulates the inherent uncertainty and unpredictability of the quantum factor."[50])

Human consciousness, then, is the only receptor which can accept the information of the quantum wave without consciousness itself as a receptor possessing a quantum behavior which influences the reception of the information. Only if human consciousness has a completely different behavior from every other existent thing in the universe (if it is something different even from the function of the brain as an organ of measurement and verification), only then does a resolution of the measurement problem of quantum physics immediately suggest itself.[51] Thanks to consciousness, measurement gives rise to information which is final and common to every bearer of consciousness. It constitutes an "apprehension" which is a product of an interaction between consciousness and the brain, but is not determined by physical brain function[52] – and only then is objective reality formed.

This manifestly ontological interpretation, which arises from quantum physics, allows no latitude for the identification of the real and the existent with the arbitrary subjectivism of human individual impressions. It nevertheless constitutes an interpretation of the real which is incompatible with the Newtonian demand for objective verification. Reality, for quantum physics, is constituted by the *participation* of the human being in it. Without an active encounter between human consciousness and quantum information – an encounter between the human *logos* and the *logos* of nature – no existent reality is formed. The existential fact is the encounter itself, not something apart from it.

"Every observation we make is equivalent to a quantum measurement"[53] which constitutes a real verification only when it acquires a specific value, interrupting the theoretical sequence of an infinite succession of measurements. And "it is not sufficient for the result of the measurement simply to be recorded on the screen of the measuring apparatus. What is required is its recording in the consciousness of an observer. A fact consequently does not exist in its own right, but only in conjunction with its observation by a conscious observer. The observer does not play the passive role of a receptor, but becomes a participant in the phenomenon and indeed necessary to its existence."[54]

We could therefore summarize the strong anthropic principle in the following way: Every expression of reality becomes possible only through the quantum behavior of matter-energy ("When we look at photons on a large scale – much larger than the distance required for one stopwatch turn – the phenomena that we see are very well approximated by rules such as 'light travels in straight lines,' because there are enough paths around the path of minimum time to reinforce each other, and enough other paths to cancel each other out. But when the space through which a photon moves becomes too small (such as the tiny holes in the screen), these rules fail – we discover that light doesn't have to go in straight lines, there are interfaces created by two holes, and so on. The same situation exists with electrons: when seen on a large scale, they travel like particles, on definite paths. But on a small scale, such as inside an atom, the space is so small that there is no main path, no 'orbit'; there are all sorts of ways the electron could go, each with an amplitude. The phenomenon of interface becomes very important, and we have to add up the arrows to predict where an electron is likely to be."[55]) The only reality which lies "beyond" the quantum behavior of matter, and is an active receptor or partaker of the information which is conveyed by wave function, is human consciousness. Without the existence of consciousness, nothing *is* as a physical fact, since wave function (quantum information), unless it is "recorded" in consciousness, is without a value and therefore does not constitute measurement, does not localize appearance – existence – does not function as a reference in the absence of a receptor of the reference.[56]

Before we explore the implications which the "anthropic principle" might have for philosophical problems, we must return to its "weak" version. We must look briefly at the scientific arguments supporting the weak anthropic principle, at whether the weak and strong versions are complementary in determining methodological criteria for a unifying interpretation of the fact of existence in the cosmos.

We could summarize the scientific arguments supporting the weak anthropic principle by the following two statements:

1. "All natural laws, without exception, are biologically necessary. Not one is biologically superfluous. All perform a single vital biological function."[57]
2. "All the fundamental constants of nature have arbitrary arithmetical values (arbitrary in the sense that the natural laws are unable to determine them), but it is precisely these which are needed for life to develop."[58]

These aphoristic statements may be analyzed briefly in the following paradigmatic cases:

a.1 The first paradigmatic case of the biological necessity of the laws of nature is the *quantum laws*. These are the only ones that can interpret the stability of the atoms that make up matter, as a result of which the physico-chemical behavior of matter, which is indispensable for the creation of organic unions and the existence of life, is safeguarded.

Atoms, as composite systems, possess a relative stability, that is, they remain immutable provided that the energy attributed to them does not exceed a specific limit. This stability is safeguarded by the fact that not all the possible orbits of electrons around the nucleus of the atom are permissible – some are permissible and others are excluded. The choice obeys the law that "quantisizes" energy as matter. This is the law that allows electrons to undergo a change in the level of their energy without diminishing their orbital velocity.

If the diminution of the level of energy affected its velocity and slowed it down, the electron would fall unavoidably into the nucleus. In this way all the atoms would have been compressed and condensed into neutral particles of the same size as the nucleus, incapable of creating chemical bonds, more complex structures, biochemical unions, living organisms.[59]

"The primary presupposition of life is the existence of matter with a stable physico-chemical behavior. Stable atoms and particles can exist only if the fundamental and constant changes in their state are hindered. And this can take place physiologically only if we accept the 'quantisization' of energy, which leads in turn to the wave-particle duality of matter hypothesis and its probabilistic interpretation. The quantum laws are therefore not a caprice of nature but a necessity constitutive of a cosmos in which the phenomenon of life would be fundamentally possible."[60]

a.2 The second paradigmatic case of the biological necessity of the laws of nature is the *a priori* principle of the *composite character of atomic nuclei.*

If the nuclei of atoms were not composite but unitary or symbolic, the only source of energy production in the universe would have been the chemical reactions provoked by the action of the electrons that orbit around the nucleus. Chemical reactions release a very limited amount of energy. If the sun of our planetary system emitted heat and light only as a result of chemical combustion, it would have exhausted its reserves of energy within a period of 5,000 years.

The time necessary, however, for the appearance of life on our planet was one billion years. The sun then would have used a source of energy six or seven times more productive than the usual chemical reactions, so that its emission of rays could be extended by the same factor – that is to say, from thousands of years to billions of years.

The splitting of the atomic nucleus produces energy six or seven times greater than that produced by chemical combustion, that is, precisely what is needed for astral bodies to release energy not for thousands but billions of years, and for the appearance and sustenance of life.[61]

a.3 The third paradigmatic case of the biological necessity of the law of nature is the *laws of the linked action of strong and weak nuclear forces*.

The nuclei of atoms are composite. They consist of protons and neutrons. Today we know that even protons and neutrons are composite, consisting of quarks. For quarks to be held together as unities of protons and neutrons and for protons and neutrons to be held together as unities of atomic nuclei – to be held together in such infinitely small distances in spite of their electrostatic repulsions and in spite of their tremendous kinetic energy on account of the uncertainty principle[62] – very strong forces of interaction between them are required. These are the so-called *strong nuclear forces* – indeed the strongest forces that exist in nature.

There are also, however, *weak nuclear forces*: these are the forces that make possible the transformation of protons into neutrons and neutrons into protons. This transformation, and the splitting of unstable nuclei which it provokes, is the reason for the existence of radioactivity and the thermonuclear chain reactions which take place in the matter that makes up the astral bodies.

The linked action of strong and weak nuclear forces ensures the energy which is produced by nuclear fission, an energy, as we have seen, which is indispensable for the appearance and maintenance of life.

The magnitude of these forces and their linking produce precisely those values which determine the presuppositions for the existence of life: If the strong nuclear forces were somewhat weaker, the formation of composite nuclei would not have been possible. In the universe only hydrogen would have existed and perhaps helium – the heavier elements of the sun would have been missing and with them the carbon which is a fundamental constituent of living matter. The variety of chemical unions which are indispensable for life would have been lacking.

If, on the contrary, the strong nuclear forces had been somewhat stronger, then all the hydrogen would have been transformed into heavy elements, and in the first minutes after the Big Bang. As a result, there would have been none of the nuclear energy which is released by the "combustion" of hydrogen (its conversion into helium) and sustains astral bodies as sources of light and heat, like the sun of our planetary system, for millions of years.[63]

Conversely, if the weak nuclear forces were even weaker, the "combustion" of hydrogen would also have been correspondingly weaker. Because the intermediate stage for converting hydrogen into helium is the production of deuterium, which is due to the slow action of the weak nuclear force (in splitting neutrons into protons, electrons and neutrinos). If this action were weaker, the splitting of neutrons could not have taken place, the production of deuterium would have been impossible, and consequently the "combustion" of hydrogen would have been prevented, that is to say, the most important source of nuclear energy, which is indispensable in the long cosmic process of preparation for the appearance and sustenance of life.

If, on the other hand, the weak nuclear forces had been somewhat stronger, then their splitting of neutrons would have been faster and the sun of our planetary system would have exploded like a vast hydrogen bomb a few minutes after the Big Bang. Thus there would have been no hydrogen once again, whose "combustion" creates the conditions indispensable for life.[64]

To the fundamental constants of nature and their arbitrary arithmetical values, which are precisely what is needed for the emergence of life, could be added, still very briefly, the following paradigmatic cases:

b.1 The first paradigmatic case, *the values of the constants of particles*.

The masses of the elementary particles are fundamental constant quantities, whose values are clearly dependent upon each other. Their values in themselves cannot be determined on the basis of the knowledge of the laws of nature or other natural parameters. They appear as independent and free from every natural context of measurement. They are naturally "arbitrary," but they do not cease to be constants. If they were not what they are or were changed in the slightest degree, the whole structure of the microcosms and the macrocosm would have been very different.

We determine the values of the masses of particles on the basis of a conventional unit of atomic mass, which is defined as one twelfth of the atom of carbon. In this way we ascertain with precise experimental methods that the neutron, for example, is a little heavier than the proton. And that the difference between the mass of the proton and the mass of the neutron is greater than the mass of the electron. We confirm that these given differences constitute decisive presuppositions for the existence and sustenance of the phenomenon of life. Specifically:

If the mass of the neutron were not bigger than the mass of the proton, the interactions between the weak nuclear forces would not be what they are. They would have been different, with the result that even the proton (the basic structural building block of nuclear matter) would have been transformed into an unstable particle with a much smaller life span. We know experimentally that the life span of protons depends upon the difference in the mass of the neutron compared with the mass of the proton, and also upon the constant for the couplings of weak interactions.[65] A shorter proton life span, however, would have rendered the existence of stable atoms of hydrogen impossible, and consequently the production of nuclear energy (light and heat) which is ensured by the fusion of hydrogen would be equally impossible.

According to our present state of knowledge, "nothing compels the mass of the neutron to be bigger than the mass of the proton. Its value is an independent free parameter. Yet whether life came into existence or not in the universe was dependent on this choice."[66]

The same is true for the value of the mass of the electron: If the mass of the electron had been greater than the difference between the mass of the neutron and the mass of the proton, the interactions between weak nuclear forces would again have been altered. In this case the splitting of the neutron, which is controlled by these forces, would consequently have been impossible in terms of energy. The free neutron would no longer have been an unstable particle, but a stable one, like the proton. In that case the slow activity of the weak nuclear force would not have been sufficient for the splitting of the neutron, and consequently there would have been no production of deuterium, which, as we have seen, is the intermediate stage for the transformation of hydrogen into helium, that is, for the "combustion" of hydrogen.

"If one were to make an extensive study of the problem of 'nuclear fusion' (on this planet and in the stars), one would see that the inequality of the difference between the mass of the neutron – mass of the proton and the mass of the electron is of vital significance for the structure of our world and the biological suitability of the universe."[67]

b.2 The second paradigmatic case, *the constants linking the fundamental fields*.

In classic physics we call a "field" the area covered by the forces exercised by a particle – electromagnetic, gravitational and nuclear forces. Quantum physics introduces a unifying overview of particles, forces and fields. The concept of the wave-particle in quantum physics unifies nature (mass) and energy (wave-force) in the single reality of the quantum field. The quantum field theory, in conjunction with the correlative definitions of position-space (particle) and speed-time (wave), describes the interaction between waves, that is, between the active forces which are exercised by particle masses.

We speak of stable combinations of the fundamental fields with reference to the constant values produced by linking the three basic forces: the electromagnetic, the gravitational and the nuclear. The forces of gravity, for example, increase in proportion to mass. They must therefore be exceptionally weak, otherwise their strength on the macroscopic level would have been so great that matter would have collapsed under the influence of its accumulated gravitational attraction. But it is insufficient that they are weaker in themselves – it is insufficient for the appearance and preservation of life. In order for life to exist, the gravity constant must be in precisely the required ratio to the electromagnetic forces constant:

Their ratio is: 1 to 10^{40}. If the value of the gravity constant in relation to the electromagnetic energy constant's value were to change from 10^{-40} to 10^{-39} (an insignificant change one would say), then the luminosity of the stars, that is, the frequency on which they radiate energy into space, would have been increased by a factor of one million – their nuclear fuel would have been consumed at a rate one million times faster. But then they would have been exhausted much sooner. The time margins necessary for the appearance and preservation of life would not have existed.

This same relationship may also be considered from the perspective of the constant values of electromagnetic activity: If the ratio of the electromagnetic forces to the forces of gravity were altered even in the slightest, if they were 2 to 10^{-40} or -1 to 10^{-40}, the entasis of the sun's radiation would have been either so great that it would have hindered the creation of organic unions, or so constricted that the organic particles would not have the necessary freedom of movement for the formation and preservation of complex living organisms.

"In the same way, one could examine the significance of the arithmetical values of the constants linking the other fundamental fields for the structure of the cosmos too. And the result may be anticipated: Their values are within the very narrow limits that make our existence possible."[68]

The scientific arguments supporting the weak version of the anthropic principle are not exhausted by examples illustrating the biological appropriateness of nature's laws and fundamental constants. They also refer to a number of other assertions of contemporary physics, of which I shall set out, by way of example, two more:

I. The reality of the universe consists of particles and antiparticles, of matter and anti-matter. The total quantities of these two givens can never be balanced, because they would simply annihilate each other in an explosion of intense light which would leave no residue.

There is therefore a given quantitative difference between particles and anti-particles of every kind, with matter clearly enjoying a supremacy over anti-matter – matter is in an appreciable majority, and from this the galaxies, the individual heavenly bodies and the terrestrial living organisms are constructed.

This quantitative superiority of matter is dependent upon a very precise subatomic equilibrium: the asymmetry between "baryon number" and "lepton number."

"Baryons" is the name given to heavy nuclear particles, such as the proton, the neutron and the so-called mesons – particles to which, in accordance with the quantum theory of gravity, gravitational force-energy is attributed. "Leptons" is the name given to light non-nuclear particles such as the electron, the muon and the neutrino.

If we give a baryon number zero to the photon and the leptons (which have zero mass and consequently do not exert any gravity) and a baryon number +1 to the baryons, we must correspondingly give a lepton number zero to baryons and a lepton number +1 to the leptons. Their anti-bodies would have identical but negative values: the anti-baryons would have the baryon number -1 and the anti-leptons the number -1.

Significantly, these numbers are conserved in the most precise balance in the interactions of the elementary particles. That is to say, the sum total of the baryon number or lepton number is identical on both sides of a particle interaction. Which means, among other things, that the baryons and the anti-baryons, the leptons and the anti-leptons can be created or destroyed only as pairs.

This very precise conservation of the sum total of the baryon and lepton number in every particle interaction conserves the values of these numbers, which are stable within the universe as a whole, without their ever being canceled out. If they were canceled out, the same quantity of particles and anti-particles of every kind would have existed, in which case their complete canceling out would have supervened even from the first moments of the Big Bang.[69]

II. The modern illusion that humanity can have an "objective" view of the world was always accompanied by a question relating to the absurdity of the existence of an infinite universe: "that this whole vast construction exists simply for [...] insignificant creatures like ourselves."[70] This "stumbling block" is transformed by contemporary physics into a hermeneutic presupposition for the understanding of the reality of the universe: We possess clear scientific indications that even the size of the universe is precisely that which is required for life to exist on the tiny planet Earth, for intelligent conscious beings to come into existence.

More specifically, for life to be created from inanimate matter about one billion years are needed. Consequently, a universe is presupposed which can endure for at least this length of time. The parameters of this necessary time-sequence are three: the total mass of the universe, the speed of light (since the general theory of relativity plays a part in the action) and the constant of universal attraction. To balance the chronological duration of the universe required for life with its presupposed parameters, the total mass of the universe must assume the numerical value which is precisely equivalent to the scientifically established factual datum: 10^{54} gr.

We know that our galaxy has a hundred billion suns like our own and that in the visible universe there are roughly another ten billion similar galaxies. We estimate that in the universe as a whole there are 10^{21} suns. If the universe were to contain only 10^{18} suns, the appearance of life on our tiny planet would have been impossible. A comparatively slight reduction in the total mass of the universe, a universe with "only" 10^{18} suns, would have been too small to "contain" the phenomenon of life. [71]

The conclusions to which the "anthropic principle" of contemporary physics necessarily leads us open up a complex problem for philosophy. But the clarification – or just the description – of the various aspects of the problem is not easy. In the first place a very broad assimilation of quantum physics' specialized language and methodological approaches is required. The chief difficulty, however, seems to be located on another level: The philosophical problem which the "anthropic principle" presents is radically incompatible with modern people's mentality and established habits of thought.

Every scientific assertion, however well founded, which possibly refers – even indirectly and hypothetically – to a non-materialistic interpretation of what exists, and more especially of human existence and consciousness, seems to provoke the automatic psychological resistance of modern humanity: the resistance of a latent anxiety about the slightest possible reference to metaphysical suppositions. It is a theme that could well be studied by the science of social psychology. Even if the metaphysical possibility emerges from the strictest scientific research, it tends to be ignored in practice, to be consigned to silence if it cannot be obliterated – it creates psychological insecurity, threatens the entire rational organization of human life in modernity. It is unintelligible to the mentality and established habits of thought of modern humanity to allow space for the philosophical elaboration of metaphysical possibilities.

Thus philosophy finds it difficult to exploit the problem presented by the "anthropic principle" in a fruitful way. Only by going outside the aims and priorities of modernity can the conclusions which contemporary physics obliges us to accept be exploited philosophically. The priorities of modernity are centered on cognition theory, which is why the radical revolution in the field of contemporary physics is followed, up to a point, by the epistemological branch of philosophy. But any extension of philosophical problematics to possible ontological conclusions which imply non-materialist suppositions encounters *a priori* rejection by both philosophers and others.

Modernity works with the associations of the past. For this reason every non-materialist interpretation of what exists refers self-evidently to the idealist metaphysics prominent in the western European past. This metaphysics worked with absolutized mental categories of the Euclidean and Newtonian version of what really exists. Accordingly, the anti-metaphysical hostility of modern humanity always set the naïve positivism of Euclidean and Newtonian empiricism against metaphysical idealism. Thus in both cases, the problems presented by the "anthropic principle" of contemporary physics demand the transcendence of Euclidean and Newtonian associations, a liberation from the cosmological presuppositions and the cognitive indisputabilities of European metaphysics and anti-metaphysics. That is why one could maintain, in a non-arbitrary manner, that the extension and development of the philosophical problem of the "anthropic principle" signals the transition to a postmodern philosophy.

The "anthropic principle" and especially quantum physics call for the rejection of modernity's self-evident and established attitude towards the "objective" observation of nature. For modern humanity, an "extrinsic" theory of an objective cosmic completeness in itself is interwoven with the very concept of science and scientific observation. This self-evident and presupposed attitude can coexist with the incontrovertible principle of the theory of relativity, that the fact of the observer influences and shapes the results of the observation. This compatibility is possible because it does not destroy the distinction between the subjectivity of the observer and the objectivity of what is observed. But the demand of quantum physics that we should regard human consciousness as a term and presupposition for the very existence of cosmic reality shifts the meaning of what exists and what is real away from the phenomenology of given entities: It identifies the verification of what exists with the dynamic of an active *relationship*, not a relationship between subject and object, but the dynamic assertion of relativity as a primary element for constituting not only the subject but also the signifier of the cosmos.

Human consciousness within the context of quantum physics (and particularly of the "measurement problem") is proved to be the initial "place" where the cosmic signifier is formed into an existential fact. Consciousness itself is not defined by the terms of the operation of the cosmic fact, by the terms of quantum mechanics, which is why consciousness is distinguished from the brain and its functioning, even though the brain and consciousness interact and mutually affect each other.

Such a version of consciousness, which makes its metaphysical character obligatory for science, understandably, so far as modern humanity is concerned, refers to what the metaphysics of the European past has called the *soul* – a concept on whose rejection, or materialistic interpretation, almost the entire structure of modernity has been based. "Now we find that physics," as Alastair Rae observes in *Quantum Physics*, "previously considered the most objective of all sciences, is reinventing the need for the human soul and putting it right at the centre of our understanding of the universe!"[72] To what extent, however, the concept of the "soul," as it has been understood within the context of a transcendental idealism, is compatible with the meaning of consciousness presupposed by quantum physics is one of the key problems of transition to a postmodern philosophy.

To recapitulate, for philosophical conclusions to be drawn from the contemporary synthesis of physics and ontology, of physics and metaphysics, a bold fundamental change of the linguistic code is needed: the liberation of philosophical language from associations referring to earlier metaphysical intellectualism, or mystical arbitrariness, or positivistic naivité.

If physics offers a pragmatological basis for the impossibility of separating existential fact from its cognitive verification, if human consciousness-cognition is a condition-presupposition for the quantum and therefore the total cosmic fact constituted as an existential given, then the fundamental linguistic signifiers of the real and existent would need the redefinition of concepts such as *relation* and *reason* and the presupposition on which they are founded, the *person*.

Relation, in this perspective, is not simply the "extrinsic" mental relationship between objects. It is not a phenomenological sequentiality, order and functional combination, assembled from observation, convergence, encounter, exchange or parallel operations. Nor is it simply a syntactic structure, an effective combination or a complementary reciprocity. Relation is fundamentally referentiality as the exclusive *mode* of formation of the existential fact – from the quantum composition of the behavior of matter, as the active formation of the human subject by means of reason "in the field of the Other"[73] – with the "horizon" or recipient of the reference as a given.

The quantum fact is a fact of relation, created as an existential given only with reference to the consciousness-cognition of the subject. The subject "precedes" the relation as a term in order for the quantum referentiality to be created as a fact of relation, as a fact of existence. That which "precedes," however, as a term in order that the relation should be created, already possesses the referentiality of the term of the relation, that is, itself exists in the mode of the reference.

In this same hermeneutic perspective I call *logos* or *reason* the indicator of the reference: the indicator of the *mode*, of the aim, of the cause, of the active response – the indicator of the emergence of what exists into a relation with the subject. The otherness of every referential manifestation is also the otherness of reason: Reason "informs" the cognitive relation, defines and unifies the comparativeness of relations which are presupposed by the marking of otherness – reason creates an otherness of relation indicative of formal-modal differentiations in that which exists.

Finally, the word *person* is the linguistic term which I use to signify the subject not as an existential given in itself, but as an active fact of reference and relation, and at the same time as a "horizon" manifesting the referentiality of existential things. The Greek word for "person," *prosopon*, is a compound word formed from the prefix *pros* (towards) and the noun *ops* (face) (*opos* in the genitive). Person (*prosopon*) signifies a referential act: I have my face-towards someone or something. I am opposite. In contrast with the word "individual" (*atomon*), which reveals a static existential unit, wholly homogeneous in itself, the person has no being except as-towards a second term of the relations which it realizes.

The active referentiality of every person arises from relationship as an existential fact which is unique, dissimilar and unrepeatable – the person is recognized as existential otherness by means of the "rational" otherness of the relations which it has realized. At the same time it is the only existence which defines itself as subjective self-consciousness. That which defines itself is distinguished from its capacity to define, and for this reason even subjective self-consciousness refers to an indefinable "nucleus"[74] of personal otherness, a nucleus which transcends reason, since the hypostatic potentiality of reason is the existential presupposition or term of the relation. The ineffable (not strictly definable) *hypostasis* (or real existence) of the human person is the only existential reality in the world which is not exhausted in the referentiality of relation, in quantum referentiality, although it is recognized and defined only by means of the relation.

On the basis of these summary definitions of the signifiers *relation*, *reason*, *person* and *hypostasis*, we can conclude this chapter with the following summary:

If the "anthropic principle" and quantum physics offer a pragmatological basis for the impossibility of distinguishing the existential fact from its cognitive verification, if human consciousness-cognition is a term-presupposition for the quantum and therefore the entire fact of the world to be constituted as an existential fact, then every reality is recapitulated in the relationship of humanity with an active reason (*logos*) as an *invitation-to-relationship*, which is directed towards humanity alone.

The fact of the world constitutes reality only because there exists the human recipient of the world's invitatory reason – the reality of the world is created only by its being an invitation-to-relationship, regardless of whether it refers to the existence of that which is invited.

If reality – not as a subjective impression, but as scientifically verified nature – is an active invitation-to-relationship, then the semantics of the "anthropic principle" and, more generally, of quantum physics, is able to clarify what we have always called the world's *beauty*. This reference has the character of inviting to relationship and is constitutive of personal relationship – "as calling all things to itself, which is why it is called beauty."[75]

If what exists cannot be known as an objective *something*, but only as an active *how*, if we study our relationship with the world's presupposed referentiality to cosmic becoming – the active invitatory character of the world's *logos* – then the possibility of connective intentionalities of the universe, as in the "weak anthropic principle," is freed from the dilemma of either necessity or chance. The biological appropriateness of natural laws and constants accords with the invitatory function of the world's becoming, which is an existential fact only with reference to the human person, the recipient of the cosmopoeic invitation.

In that case, even the formation of the universe "before" the appearance of its human cognition does not destroy the character of being invited-to-relationship of the universe's referentiality. For the "before" and the "after" are by-products of the relationship between humanity and the world, the only relationship that constitutes an existential fact and whatever "pre"-required evolutionary process is needed for its realization.[76]

If the fact of the world constitutes a reality as an invitation-to-relationship, then physics and metaphysics are both implied in the unified fact of a dialogue: The dialogue is formed by the rational recipient of the world's reason (*logos*) and the causal principle of invitatory reason (*logos*). The dialogue (*dia-logos*) is an existential fact – the given existence of the world as regards humanity – and demands that both terms of the dialogue's relationship should exist. If reality exists only as an invitation-to-relationship, the invitation, referring to relationship, cannot refer to its invitatory character alone, denying any real content to the relationship. Which means that the invitatory character of the world's *logos* does not invite a relationship simply with the world itself.

The quantum constitution of the world constitutes an existential fact which refers only to human consciousness-cognition. It does not form an objective *something*, a hypostatic term of a relation. The quantum wave acquires value and constitutes an existential signification only in its encounter with human consciousness. "Outside" this encounter it is not signed as an existential fact. That is why we also say that the quantum wave is a rational principle (*logos*) that calls into relationship, but not a term that brings the relationship into being. A hypostatic term (with the relation given as an existential fact) is the causal principle of the invitatory rational principle (*logos*) of the world, not as a logical consequence but as a "value" (existential verification) of the first term of the existential relationship.

The human relationship with the causal principle of the world's invitatory *logos*, though it creates the existential reality of the world, does not entail the obligatory affirmation of the relationship by humankind. What is obligatory or inescapable is the encounter of humanity with the world's rational principle (*logos*) (the consciousness-cognition of quantum referentiality). But the attribution of an invitatory character to the world's rational principle (*logos*) – the acknowledgement of this principle as an invitation-to-relationship – is a *personal* fact (as is every affirmation in an invitation-to-relationship). It belongs to the freedom of the person to define itself as the second term of a relationship, to acknowledge or to deny and reject the invitation-to-relationship.

Unawareness of the invitation, the denial or rejection of the relationship, does not destroy the invitatory character of the world's rational principle (*logos*). But it leaves the rational invitation suspended without reference to the first term of the relationship (to the causal principle of the invitation). The dialogue (encounter) between the human rational principle and that of the world inevitably makes the world an existential fact, but the rejection or denial of the world's invitation-to-relationship reveals the world's existence to be meaningless and without purpose. The world appears as an autonomous, causeless and aimless fact to human consciousness, the rational principle (*logos*) of the world refers to the ontologically uninterpretable, to the meaninglessness of nothingness or chance.

Consequently, the human person, as recipient of the world's rational principle (*logos*), does not come to consciousness of self and does not function as a term constitutive of a relationship. Humanity interprets its existence as a marginal happening brought about in the universe by chance, a product of coincidental configurations of material becoming, as a causeless and aimless product. Its conscious cognition may prove to be a term-presupposition so that the fact of the world can be formed into an existential given, but this assertion refers simply to the relativization of scientific knowledge or, more radically, to an agnostic subjectivism and skepticism.

No metaphysical argument can force a human being to enter into a personal relationship with the personal existence of the world's causal principle. The freedom of the person – of existential self-determination which is definitive of personal hypostasis – precedes and determines the cognitive conclusions from the experience of relationship or from the rejection of relationship. For this reason, not even the "anthropic principle" of contemporary physics, in spite of its metaphysical "charge" and the clearly ontological proposition which it entails, can function as apodictic metaphysical proof.

Thesis 2

The Modal Sense Of The Infinite And The Absolute

1. The experience of the modally infinite

The word *infinite* refers to the mental conception of an expanse without limits. The conception is fundamentally mental because it emerges from sensory experience only by analogy. It is also without question metaphysical, since "nature flies from the infinite; for the infinite is imperfect and nature always seeks an end."[1] The "perfected" and the limited, definition and limitation, are basic premises of the empirical knowledge that we have of nature.

Sensory experience, however, still leads us by a process of abstraction to the mental conception of the infinite. And this experiential starting point for the mental process of abstraction permits a personal "sensing" of the infinite, especially in the following three cases: When we gain a sense of the infinity of time (that the "duration of time is limitless"[2] – "infinity is present in time"[3]), or of the infinity of numbers ("limited as well as indefinitely numerous"[4] – "infinite in number by addition"[5]), or of the infinity of space or expanse ("the infinity of distance"[6]).

Of course all three cases relate to one and the same "sensing" of the possible extension of measurement to infinity – of numbers, of time and of space. We conceive of infinite progressive enumeration, temporal duration and spatial distance only "by sensing" the possibility, not as a representational reality. And we conceive of the infinite, in these cases, as a quantitative category. The meaning of "infinite" refers us to the "sensing" of unlimited size, of "indeterminate" (unbounded) expanse.

The word *infinite* acquires a qualitative significance as metaphor and to convey subjective experiences – always, however, as a quantitative category, as a definition of unlimited dimensions: "It is of the nature of desire to be unlimited," we read in Aristotle;[7] "indefinitely aggravating their injustice," notes Plato;[8] and Pindar speaks of "infinite darkness."[9]

We could also define a third meaning of "infinite" on the basis of the immense variety of the *modes* in which a natural fact is presented to human experience – the limitless scale of what differentiates the subject's relationship with every specific existent thing. It would be helpful in this case to speak of a *modal* meaning of the infinite, a meaning which affords a more immediate experiential "sensing" of what is signified by the word:

We possess an immediate experiential knowledge of the infinite range of what differentiates the *mode* of existence: the countless distinct individual units in every uniform whole, the boundless variety of *modes* in which the same natural fact can operate. We possess – above all – knowledge of the infinite possibilities manifested by the *relationship* of every human subject with every specific expression of the real and the existent. We experience the indeterminable distinctness and dynamic novelty of the *mode* of every existential fact, experiencing the comparatively absolute otherness of every combination of circumstances which determine our relationship with what exists.

You could say that in these cases the experiential "sensing" of the infinite and the indeterminate is not established quantitatively by addition, but rather experientially by abstraction: The infinity of possibilities is summarized in the experience of verifying unique otherness – the comparative presuppositions of otherness converge by abstraction towards a positive knowledge of individual distinctiveness. The "sensing" of the infinite is not located in the conscious ability to extend measurement to infinity, but is a sensing of the summary abstraction of metrical progression in the peculiar mode, or uniqueness, of every relationship.

It is evident that the *modal* meaning of the infinite presupposes nature but also transcends nature – transcends the phenomenology of the finite through experiencing the limitless *modes* of the expression of finitude. This is an experience of the *logos*-mode of nature's existence and, accordingly, a "sensing" of a transition to a metaphysics concerning the indeterminacy and infinity of relations created by the "rationality" of the world's *mode*. The modal meaning of the infinite refers to the metaphysical indeterminacy of the possible "rational" expression of what exists – to the infinity of ever unique, distinct and unrepeatable expressions of rational reciprocity which belongs to the relationship between humanity and the world.

In terms of the themes and language of post-Newtonian physics, the meaning of the infinite often appears to be more modal than quantitative.

Let us by way of example go back to the hypothesis that the universe as a whole is limited (is not infinite), but is also without terminal boundaries (is consequently indeterminate): The infinite may be expressed not in unlimited dimensions, but as a *mode* of interpreting the finite which permits the transcendence of its finiteness.

Another analogy is the infinite curvature of space-time or the infinite density of matter in "black holes" in space – as also at the moment of the universe's initial Big Bang. This is a formulation which presents the infinite not as a metrical series that extends forever but as an increasing abstraction of measurement which is finally summed up in a version of the finite in which values are extended to infinity.

A further analogy is the infinite (never surmountable) difference between the position and velocity of two similar particles in subatomic space, the absolute exclusion of their coincidence, as predicted by Pauli's exclusion principle. Or, furthermore, the state of the void (absolute vacuum) which quantum field theory posits as a state of complete nothingness, nevertheless "creative" of all the actual processes of the field. These are formulations which present the infinite as a non-predetermined exclusion of infinite possibilities, or as an active transcendence of all possible values defining any existential fact whatsoever.

Through many analogous expressions and formulations, contemporary physics permits philosophical reflection to conceive of the infinite not as a mental ascent to an immeasurable quantitative vastness, but as an "experiential" concept, in that it leads to our conscious realization of a *mode of existence* with an unlimited dynamic of possible manifestations or contraction of every manifestation. A mode which abolishes or transcends measurement by excluding any measure defining its dynamic or permitting unlimited values.

Of course, such an interpretation of the infinite remains incompatible with modernity's demand for "objectivity." Because it includes the recipient of the interpretation as one of its defining factors. If the theory of relativity obliges us to include the observer's presence as a factor shaping both the fact and the result of the observation, its actual consequences lead us necessarily to the entailment of the infinite as the *modal* determination of the possibilities of the relationship between the observer and what is observed.

And without doubt in certain cases the presence (position and motion) of the observer may be considered a measurable factor in the result of the observation. But it is impossible for the modal infinity of possibilities for "rational" relationship between observer and what is observed to be subjected to any kind of measurement whatsoever. This modal infinity has a clearly ontological content: it refers to the metaphysical indeterminacy of "rational" manifestations of what exists and of the *personal* otherness of the human observer.

If knowledge of reality is formed as a fact of *relationship* between observer and what is observed, then the involvement of the observer in the fact of the observation relativizes the result of the partial observation, demonstrating the indeterminacy of the possible relations between observer and things observed. The observer is not a detached observation unit, a partial "prism" for the scrutiny of what is observed, but an actively knowing subject, that is, a determinative term of the modal infinity of the possible relations with what is observed. That is why every observation is a self-cognition experience of the *personal* mode of existence of the subject, a mode which permits the cognitive coordination of the observer with the modal infinity of the universe – it demonstrates the human freedom of the relationship as a genuine experience of the modal absolute.

The inclusion of the *personal* mode of human existence in the analysis of the fact of scientific observation (the interpretation of the *relationship* between observer and what is observed as a fundamentally existential possibility which is infinite in a modal sense) transforms the terms of the experiential interpretation of the real and existent, and also of the physical and metaphysical: The real and the physical are not just what is established through measurement but are extended as experience of the modally absolute – an experience of the *mode* of active manifestation accessible only to the undetermined dynamic of the *relationship*. As a real and physical fact, the human presence confirms itself, by experiencing relationship, as a modally undetermined dynamic of reference to rationality. But even the universe, being a real and physical given in its smallest and greatest dimensions, becomes known to us only as an activated *logos*, that is, by a mode of active manifestation which corresponds to the *personal* human capacity for modally undetermined rational reference. Thus what we call "reality" is a fact of metaphysical relationship between two modally infinite rational factors: the rational (personal) existence of humanity and the rationally (in the mode of personal *logos*) activated universe.

The cognitive coordination of the observer with the modal infinity of the universe demonstrates philosophically the inclusion of the dynamic of the *mode* of existence in the fact and in the result of scientific observation. The inclusion suggests the dynamic of cognition as an existential capacity for *relationship* – the capacity of limited humanity to be conscious, in its relationship with the world, of the experience of the modally infinite.

The experience of the modally infinite, however, is confirmed fundamentally not in the relationship of humanity with the world, but in its freedom from this relationship. That is, in the ability of humanity to create its own world not subject to the necessities of nature, to form relationships referring not to the facts of nature but to its own existential otherness – to create *art*, *culture*, *history*.

Modernity attributed the creation of art-culture-history to the different degree of rationality (here in the sense of intellectual development) which humanity exhibits in comparison with the other animals. The difference is quantitative – and consequently presents no difficulty for accepting the theory of evolution – seeing that even the animals possess some faculties of reason and consciousness. The rational capacities of animals are driven chiefly by the instinct of self-preservation and are manifested in the relations of the animal with its natural environment: adaptation to conditions and resolution of survival problems which the environment presents. But the same could also be asserted about the manifestly superior, in a quantitative sense (i.e. more developed), intellectual capacities of human beings: they are manifested chiefly as dominion over, and utilitarian exploitation of, the natural environment – throughout the whole of human technological development.

Certainly, differences of human rationality from the rationality of animals may be taken to be a natural and not an ontological-modal difference. The radical and unbridgeable difference between human and animal (in evolutionary terms the inexplicable *leap*) may be located not in natural rationality, but in the rationality of the *freedom* from the limits of natural adaptation: in the exclusively human capacity for existential self-determination, for freedom from nature, for the creation of relationships which form a different world from what is given by nature. The active otherness of human personal creation, an otherness in relation to the "logic" and necessities of nature, the existential self-realization of subjective otherness through relations that transcend or destroy the rationality of natural adaptation, is exclusive to the human race, an infinite modal difference from the rationality of the animal. Even the contribution of contemporary psychology-psychoanalysis to the understanding of the functions of human desire and language (functions that are not subject to biological necessity and to the instinct of self-preservation[10]) should be sufficient to prove the ontological-modal difference between human and animal rationality.

Modernity's materialistic positivism insisted that even escaping from natural adaptation – the creation of art, culture, history – is an evolutionary consequence of the genetically predetermined intellectual capacities of humanity. Positivism has maintained that on the level of this high intellectual development, the typically animal instinct of self-preservation is expressed as "valuations of power," clothed in the illusion of a freely willed "decision" and in the utilitarian establishment of "regulative principles of behavior." The external appearances of independent "decisions" and the utilitarian necessity for regulative principles are legitimized psychologically by elevating them to the status of "values" and by accounting for their causality by claiming a fictional transcendental origin[11] – creating in this way the "superstructure" which we accept as "culture."

But on the basis of the criteria and logic of materialistic positivism, although we can interpret human culture up to a point as a "superstructure" erected upon natural necessity, it is impossible for us to interpret those aspects of culture which stand in opposition to natural rationality or even overturn it. Although the rationality of animals always tends to value that which is a given of nature, the freedom of human beings is located precisely in the actual break with natural givenness, in their need to put together "from nothing," if it were possible, their own creation.

What we call "culture" is the very dynamic of human freedom which in a practical way transforms the terms of natural rationality: It overturns or even denies the adaptation of humanity to nature, and can even arrive at the destruction of nature as given for the sake of the human goal. Humanity cuts itself off from nature – as if it did not itself belong to nature – with a view to responding to the need for freedom from nature, a freedom which constitutes it as a subject. The masterpieces of human art emerge from this dynamic rebellion against adaptation to nature, as do the astounding technological achievements, which – in the latter case – destroy the logic of the "superstructure" and carry threats of universal ecological disaster, such as those which accompany the end of modernity.

Humanity's freedom from nature is at all events relative since human beings are themselves naturally limited existences. But the original material which human beings transform into an expression of their existential otherness, is also a given of nature. Both human existence with its creative activity and the material of human creations are subject to the limitations of nature as given – limitations, at least, of place, time, decay and death.

Absolute freedom for human beings would consist in their creating not only the initial matter of their creations, but even the existential presuppositions of their nature. Only an *uncreated* existence, self-endowed with the power to determine its nature existentially and to create existent things "out of nothing" would constitute absolute and infinite freedom.

In spite of all this, even *created* humanity has some experience of creation "out of nothing" through the *modes* in which given physical matter is used. With regard to the *mode* of the activity, humanity seems able to set out from nothing: to establish *modes* of its subjective expression "from nothing." Even humanity's subjective existential otherness may be self-defined as *modes* of using its natural abilities which are not naturally predetermined.

In this way, on the level of *mode* of activity, human freedom becomes a fundamental condition of the experience of the infinite and the unlimited. It is at least an experience of potentiality, a practical sensing that humanity can transcend or destroy the *modes* of nature: that it can establish unique, distinct and unrepeatable *modes* of expression-manifestation of its real otherness.

As a potentiality, of course, the human experience of infinite and unlimited *modal* freedom implies an ability to act, subject to limitations: limitations in the insufficiency of natural human capacities and limitations in the "resistance" of physical matter to being subjected completely to human action of the primary mode. In spite of all this, the experience of the modally infinite may be regarded as real and not imaginary, because it is an experience of the unlimited dynamic of relationship, unencumbered by the limited character of the terms of the relationship.

The experience of the modally unlimited is not just the intellectual cognition of infinite possible modes. It is located principally in the freedom of humanity from the conditions-modes of nature.

A painter uses naturally pigmented materials in order to present a natural object. This representation, however faithful to the original, conveys a unique, distinct and unrepeatable (i.e. *personal*) relationship with the object. Certainly it conveys one of the infinite possible ways of regarding the object. But at the same time the artist's representation also conveys his or her freedom from every naturally possible way of regarding (freedom from the infinite ways in which the object could be photographed): It conveys that act of regarding which refers immediately to the expressive uniqueness and distinctness of the artist himself or herself – the artist's representation of the object is a *logos* of the artist, a manifestation of his or her *personal* otherness, his or her own free personal relationship with the object.

Accordingly – as Heidegger[12] observed from a different viewpoint – every work of art is an allegory (in the etymological sense of the word): it expresses-speaks of something different from the physical reality of the work of art. It reveals the existential otherness of the artist, his or her freedom from adaptation to the terms of nature. Every work of art refers to meta-nature, not to nature.

In the relationship between humanity and the world, the two terms or factors of the relationship (humanity and the matter of nature) are clearly limited – they have limited possibilities for existence and energy. The dynamics of their relationship, however, are clearly (i.e. experientially) unbounded: Humanity establishes *personal* relationships with nature (free from the restrictions of nature). But even nature, at least as revealed by its quantum composition, operates in a *logos*-mode free from the necessity of mechanistic predeterminations, and the conditions of objectivization which human intellection imposes.

We affirm the finite power both of nature and of humanity

regarding existence and operation according to the experience of freedom or of the unbounded character of their relationship, freedom from restrictions which are imposed reciprocally by both terms of the relationship. We affirm the finiteness of the terms of the relationship on the basis of the unbounded nature of the relationship itself. The experience of the infinite and the unbounded refers to the *personal* mode of existence and operation of the human being, and to the *rational* mode in which the world exists and operates. Experiencing the finite terms of the relationship refers to the *createdness* of the nature of humanity and of the world, in their given existential and separately delineated otherness.

The poet who constructs a poem, the musician who composes a melody, the painter who creates a composition in colors, the inventor who devises an original machine, the researcher who discovers a hermeneutic principle for certain phenomena, testify experientially to the incompleteness of the final achievement compared with the dynamic universality of their original 'conception' or 'inspiration.' The experience of the relation of the artist, the inventor, the researcher, to the facts that constitute the world is unbounded in comparison with the ultimately limited meaning of this relation. The more *personal* the relation is – the more free from the limiting factors of nature – the more inexpressible it remains.

In a directly analogous manner the meaning of personal reference to the metaphysical *causal principle* of what exists is always finite and incomplete compared with experiencing the reference itself. To the degree in which the reference becomes an experience of personal *relationship*, and an experience of *reciprocity* therein, it remains beyond the powers of natural expression.

Of course, what is sought here is primarily the experiential assurance that the metaphysical causal principle really exists and not the experiential assurance that human reference is dynamically unbounded. For every mythopoeic reference to imaginary mental inventions can be modally unbounded. Only experiencing *reciprocity* in the relationship can confirm the reality of a causal principle of what exists – a *personal* Causal Principle, since only a *personal* relationship (one which is free from the limiting factors of nature) can constitute an experience of reciprocity. But such an experience, too, remains beyond the powers of natural-apodictic verification and expression.

Nevertheless, although the experience of reciprocity cannot be put into words, only the awareness of the correct (i.e. the only possible) cognitive approach to the likely metaphysical reality is of vital importance: If the *rationality* of the world refers, through the experience of the modal infinity of relationship, to a *personal* Causal Principle of the world, the assurance of the existence of such a Principle cannot be other than an experience of *reciprocity* in the relationship.

We recognize the personal Causal Principle of the world only by cultivating a relationship, not by apprehending concepts. No purely intellectual proof can confirm the existence of metaphysical reality. Only the dynamics of relationship, only the experience of reciprocity in the relationship.

No kind of personal relationship can provide us with criteria by which we can represent the reciprocity. The reciprocity, the correspondence in reality to the desired relationship, can be conceived and validated only experientially. That is why this experiential certainty is exceptionally precarious and difficult to distinguish from wishful fantasies, projections of psychological insecurity, and fond illusions.

But equally inexpressible – and equally precarious – is that experience of reciprocity or living harmony, which permits us – as only this does – to recognize, not in its immediate presence but by the indirect evidence of its activity, a real personal otherness: There are no criteria which can objectivize the difference between the art of Van Gogh and the art of

Goya, between the music of Mozart and the music of Bach, between the poetry of Eliot and the poetry of Baudelaire. Only the cultivation of our relation with the work of the artist leads us gradually to an awareness of the personal otherness of the work, which permits us to recognize and affirm this personal otherness in every new – to us – encounter with the work of the artist. We see a painting we don't know, we hear a musical composition we haven't heard before and affirm on the basis of our previous experience: this *is* Van Gogh, this *is* Mozart.

We recognize the personal Causal Principle of the world by cultivating a relationship, not by apprehending concepts. The relationship is a *personal* capacity, a capacity for freedom from the limiting factors of nature. Freedom is always a capacity, never a fixed datum. Lying in wait for us is the submission to nature's limiting factors, that is, the transformation of the relationship into a one-sided pursuit of our own natural-individual self-sufficiency: of a one-way rush towards the acquiring of individual psychological security, towards cladding ourselves in individual ideological armor, towards the embracing of individual utilitarian exploitation. So often in human history the ineffable reciprocity in the relationship between *created* and *uncreated* is transformed into an intellectualist construct, into an authoritarian institution, into an ethical system directed towards utilitarian ends.

The transformation of the metaphysical relationship into a one-sided pursuit of anthropocentric self-sufficiency limits the experience of the modally infinite to mere intellectual cognition of quantitative infinity. The individual understanding understands what it has defined as an abstractive concept that raises us up to the notion of absolute relativity and finiteness. The immensely huge, the supremely powerful, the wholly wise, the eternal are categories of quantitative reference, subject to the laws of nature, which aspire in vain to refer to metaphysical referents.

The *personal* experience of the modally infinite is primarily an experience of freedom from the laws-modes of nature. And the significance of this experience, however much it may be subject to limitation by natural powers of expression, is clearly distinguishable from intellectual abstraction. The significance of *personal* experience may be discerned, because it does not refer to specific referents, but to the dynamics of the *relation* with the referents, with the inexpressible personal otherness of the referents.[13]

The new language of post-Newtonian science seems to bring us nearer to the significance of the experience of the modally infinite, nearer to the language of art and love. This proximity allows us to propose the prerequisites for a transition from modernity to a new cultural "paradigm" – to the postmodern age.

The prerequisites of the transition are not just scientific attainments. Physicists today seek a full and coherent unified theory to embrace all the partial theories (starting with the combination of the general theory of relativity with quantum theory) and will not include arbitrarily chosen parameters adjusted *a posteriori* to achieve congruence with the facts of observation. If such a theory should be found, perhaps it would mean the end of theoretical physics, but it is not certain that it would also mean the end of modernity, the beginning of a postmodern phase in human culture. The inability of modern societies to adapt culturally to the epistemological revolution of quantum physics is a discouraging precedent which renders such a perspective probable.

The prerequisites of the transition to a postmodern cultural "paradigm" should rather be sought elsewhere. Perhaps not in a new unifying theory interpreting the given aspects of the world, but in a unifying interpretation of the "logic" of the existent and the real – unifying of the "logic" of the world, the "logic" of art, the "logic" of love. Such an interpretation cannot be theoretical: it is a human "stance," a mode of the relationship between humanity and the existent and real. And at the center of this unifying relationship is the experience of the modally infinite, that is, experiencing the *personal* mode of existence.

The human "stance" which unifies the relationship mode with the "logic" of the world, the "logic" of art, the "logic" of love, is a *personal* "stance:" It constitutes a cognitive approach to the world which does not differ from the cognitive approach to personal otherness in artistic endeavor, and an approach to the otherness of the work of art which does not differ from the dynamics of the knowledge of a person with whom one is in love.

The *personal* approach to the "logic" of the world, of art, of love presupposes the dynamic consequences of a relationship's demands: that the relationship should not be converted into a one-sided individual exploitation of its second term, to subjection and dependence, to a utilitarian seeking for advantage. Culture changes when the relationship *mode* between the human being and nature and his or her fellow human beings changes, when the *ethos* – the morality or distinctive character – of science, of art, of love is transformed.

Modernity, consistent with its medieval antecedents, has established an understanding of morality which is primarily legal and deontological. It has coupled morality with obedience to legal precepts and has detached morality from the adventure of freedom, from the dangers of relationship. Modernity has ignored the first task to be addressed for the relationship to be attained: the abandonment of a self-centered individualism, the active pursuit of self-transcendence and self-offering.

The prerequisites of the transition to a postmodern cultural "paradigm" are primarily metaphysical. They are judged fundamentally not by the further human exploitation of the laws of nature, but by the *personal* human capacity for freedom from the laws of nature.

2. The experience of the private absolute

Whether metaphysical reality can or cannot exist is not susceptible of "objective" scientific proof. But scientific proof is not the only possible way for us to approach the existent and the real. Even in the field of science, the vital hermeneutic insights and hermeneutic conceptions do not fundamentally follow the "logical path" of scientific consistency.[14] Much less are the cognitive proofs drawn from the experience of art, love, and the dynamics of linguistic communication subject to the scientific mode of operation.

The way science operates today – the language of post-Newtonian cosmology and quantum physics – seems to refer directly to metaphysical premises. But if metaphysical premises exist, they would by definition not be subject to the conditions of nature, and therefore to the definitive character which the scientific knowledge of nature, again by definition, possesses. It is clearly contradictory to pose questions about metaphysics in the terms and in the manner of physics. The very pretension of science to be definitive is incompatible with contradictory methodological choices: It is impossible to gauge weight with a measure of length, or length with a measure of weight.

Of course the metaphysical question demands definitive proofs. But this is not a demand which can be satisfied with apodictic definitions, nor can it be exhausted by scientific inquiry. Whether the world has a Causal Principle, a "sense" and intentionality, or not, the proof presupposes and entails (even as a cognitive fact) the existential *participation* of humanity in these metaphysical data or non-data. Metaphysical proof is to do with the very *mode* of human existence and knowledge, with humanity's given or possible existential powers, with the prospect of the annihilation of human existence or its liberation from the conditions of nature. The metaphysical question is literally a problem of life and death for us.

Humanity is the only existence in nature which ponders nature's boundaries. It poses questions and reflects on the possibility of metaphysical reality, it alone possessing knowledge and experience of, or even just a desire for, existential freedom from the conditions of nature. If existential freedom from the conditions of nature is possible, it is of immediate concern to humanity, it concerns us as our own probable existential potentiality. A potentiality not only for as long as humanity exists in accordance with the conditions of nature, but for real existence *beyond* the mode of nature, beyond and after biological death.

The possibility of existential freedom from nature's conditions does not obey the rules of scientific proof. The ecphrastic expression of the possibility cannot be compatible with the semantics of definition and interpretation of nature's conditions, if what is to be posited is the freedom from any logic at all of nature. Nature's logic cannot be a presupposition for the posing and investigation of the metaphysical question, only the exclusive ability of humanity to pose a question concerning freedom from nature's conditions. Only language that gives a semantic sketch of humanity's existential otherness in relation to the rest of nature can convey this exclusively human ability. A language that refers to experience of the *personal* mode of existence, to the experience of freedom from every limiting precondition – as in the experience of love, art, and the dynamics of communication.

In these sketches of the experience of *personal* existential otherness, the semantics of freedom from nature's conditions and modes suggests a fundamental transcendence of time, place and number. A possible experience of existential self-knowledge free from time, place and number clearly refers to a potential cognitive approach to the mode of *personal* existence: to freedom from nature's conditions and modes. Such a hint of personal existential potentiality may be the experience of the *private absolute*.

The experience of the private absolute hints at the potentiality of every separate human being to sense in practice, even though he or she is finite, the plenitudinous universality of all that is, to sense the partial and fragmentary as a unique, distinct and exclusive experience of the universal.

As a natural given, individual human existence is one infinitely small unit among billions of analogous existential units which exist, have existed or will exist. Every such unit is located existentially in a similarly infinitely small time interval of individual survival: an interval of some decades within the tens of thousands of years of human presence on earth and the billions of years of the life of the universe. But even in physical space, every human existential unit represents an infinitely small material presence. Such a unit occupies a habitat of a few dozen square meters; has a range of movement, these days, of some thousands of kilometers – lives, that is to say, within insignificant spatial dimensions in a universe distributed isometrically around the earth to a depth of ten billion light years.

Nevertheless, every separate human existential unit – insignificant in terms of number, time and size – experiences existence as plenitudinous universality of being: In its numerical unicity it recapitulates the numerical infinity of comparable units. It experiences the physical world as a whole as the non-dimensional space of its own unique existence. It experiences time as consciousness of the recapitulation of the past and the future in the subjective experience of historicity.

Awareness of one's own existence is for every separate human being the experience of the existential fact of the whole, the cognition of the universal potentialities of being. The world which surrounds us – the innumerable swarms of galaxies or the multitude of photons and electrons which form the universe, for all that they have pre-existed and will continue to exist regardless of our own ephemeral existence

– is the private world of subjective experience, the intimate space of our everyday life. Time which has gone before and time which will follow are the unbounded present of the historical self-consciousness of the human subject. Every partial aspect of our experience of life – pain, joy, desire, beauty, love, the grief of death – is our own cognition of the whole: all subjective love is the complete and plenitudinous reality of love; the death of a beloved person leaves all the others unmoved, but for the one who suffers the loss, it is the experience and sensation of death's universal reality.

The bounded private space of my daily life is my world. Not a partial and fragmentary microcosm, but the world in its entirety in a dimensionless and intimate immediacy of experience of the whole. This private experience of the whole can be lived within a space of some few square meters – and even within a labyrinthine complex of similar spaces – amidst a host of other private dwellings. Even there, however, within this mass of similar buildings, within this environmental uniformity, one door is my own, one door leads into my world. When I close it behind me, life, nature, history, death, love, politics, the marketplace, science, art are all summed up and completely present in the tiny and ephemeral space of my personal absolute, which I nevertheless experience as unbounded.

And why is the sense of my personal absolute not yet another psychological illusion – alongside a host of others: ideological, religious, erotic and authoritarian? Quantitative measurement and objective comparison could immediately demonstrate that any subjective feeling of universality and plenitude is fragmentary and merely relative.

Certainly the precise awareness of the universal and the plenitudinous, the experience of the personal absolute, is a fact of cognition, and as with every experience of perception, remains subject to error and illusion. In the case of the experiential cognitive fact, however, error and illusion cannot be judged and demonstrated by quantitative measurements and mental comparisons. If subjective love is a genuine experience of the universal and plenitudinous reality of love, this cannot be checked by mathematics, logic or physics. The cognitive fact of experiential knowledge is judged by standards of experiential verification. It cannot be verified by inappropriate means – that would be an arbitrary "crossing to another genus."[15]

If every experiential act of cognition is not by definition erroneous and illusory, the feeling of intimacy with the absolute, the experience of universality and plenitude, possibly constitutes a cognitive-perceptive potentiality of the subject. And then this fundamentally experiential potentiality, if only by incurring the danger of error or illusion, is a potentiality for detaching the subject from the limiting factors of the natural individual's feeling of fragmentariness, from being confined to partial and the relative experience, from the subjection of existential self-consciousness to being just another unit of nature. The experience of the private absolute is a possibility for freedom from nature's limiting factors, from reducing the cognition of existents to quantity and number, from the confining of experience to the finite and the partial. It is a potentiality for metaphysical experience.

The otherness of every human subject – its unique, distinct and unrepeatable particular physical and psychological constitution, together with its activity – is an *absolute* existential given. In Greek *apolyton*, "absolute," is connected etymologically with *apolelymenon*, "released" – detached from every predetermined similarization, unbounded with regard to the natural unit's defining similarity of form.

In the case specifically of the human subject, the otherness of its existential makeup and its existential activities is not confirmed merely *a posteriori*, merely from the observation of its phenomenology. It is also felt actively as potentiality, as an immediate experience of otherness in its relations with the surrounding world. And the experience of otherness in relations is a personal awareness of subjective existential otherness, an experience of universality and plenitude in the immediacy of the private and the intimate.

The elevation of what is private and intimate in subjective relations to the level of universality and plenitude – an empirical elevation to a level of actual experience – is a function of the absoluteness of the given otherness of relations. Every unique, distinct and unrepeatable relationship is a plenitudinous wholeness of relationship, not a section or portion of the full relationship. And as a result of this experience of plenitudinous wholeness, the subject can be aware of its existential freedom from the partial and the fragmentary, that is to say, aware of its experience of being released from the limitations of physical numerical unicity, finite temporality, and spatial location.

The active otherness of a subjective relationship, as an experience of the plenitudinous wholeness of the relationship, is a real awareness of existential freedom from nature's arithmetical, temporal and spatial limitations – it is a metaphysical experience. I repeat: How, if this is a cognitive illusion or error, can we not judge it to be so merely by whether this same relationship may or may not be transcribed into "scientific" expressions of comparative dimensions and objective measurements? The scientific approach, or the objective definition of the given aspects of a relationship, does not replace nor does it exhaust the experience itself of otherness in the relationship. The possibility that this experience is deceptive or illusory cannot be defined by scientific proof. It is judged only by the relationship's standards of authenticity or distortion.

The relationship is distorted by a unilateral individualism. It ceases to function as a dynamic of experiential knowledge when one of the terms of the relationship suggests preconditions to the cognitive consequences of the relationship, and imposes them unilaterally. If the subject's metaphysical experience of existential freedom from time, space and number – the experience of the private absolute – is a mere psychological "projection" of desire, or a psychological auto-suggestion and cocooning of the subject in pet theories and belief-systems, then the cognitive dynamic of the relationship is destroyed, the relationship is transformed into an arbitrary individualistic experience. But the possibility of distortion does not prevent the relationship from being genuine.

Is the subjective experience of freedom from time, space and number – the experience of universality and plenitude as peculiarly and intimately one's own – simply a cognitive or perceptive capacity, or does it also represents a real possibility: A possibility that the human subject can be free from the limitations of numerical specificity and finite time and space – free from death? That is the main problem.

No straight answer can be given on the basis of *a priori* epistemological assumptions subject to the laws of nature: assumptions of science, ideology, or psychology. It concerns the possible freedom of existence from the restrictions of nature, and consequently a reliance only on the experience of relationship – the only experience which holds out the possibility of release, if only cognitive and conceptual, from the restrictions of nature – can shine through and suggest a reply to the question.

3. The mode of nature and the mode of relation

Is it possible for the human subject to be structured as an existential fact on the basis of *relation* rather than *nature*? Can the fact of relationship "hypostasize" the human subject, constitute it as an existential reality?

Certainly the question cannot be answered according to cognitive precepts subject to the laws of nature: precepts of science, ideology, psychology. In our search for a language, however – a rational means of expression – to investigate the question, contemporary psychology-psychoanalysis could perhaps make a decisive contribution.

By other routes, unconnected with the problem of ontology, the science of psychology-psychoanalysis centers the human subject's initial genesis and main lines of development on the fact of relation. The aphoristic proposition: "the subject, *in initio*, begins in the space of the Other – the subject originates so long as the signifier arises in the field of the Other,"[16] emerges from positivistic research and is not hospitable to philosophical development. But as an opinion it implies the ontological problem.

If the subject originates in the Other's space, we may then make a fundamental distinction between the meanings of the terms *subject* and *biological individual*. The biological individual has an existential autonomy; it may be defined in itself. The subject not so; it may be defined only in relation to the space of the Other, in relation to the signifier's emergence in the Other's field. On the semantic level, the subject constitutes an existential fact other than and differing from the biological individual. The semantic distinction refers to experiential pragmatic proof. What we call a human *subject* is an existential reality, not without relations, but nevertheless other than and not identical with the reality of the biological individual.

We know the subject only as an active reference. The reference constituting the subject comes from a radically primary desire. "*Desidero* is the Freudian *cogito*. It is there, necessarily, [in desire] that the essential aspect of the primary process is instituted."[17] Desire appears as a presuppositional referential power which constitutes the subject, since the signifier arises in the field of the Other.

Desire is defined in the positivistic language of psychoanalytic realism as the libido, an erotic desire for a fulfilling relationship, the only relationship which (especially for humanity) transcends the biological intentionality of reproduction and constitutes "a pure instinct for life, that is to say, for immortal life, for irrepressible life, for life which has no need of any instrument, for a simplified and indestructible life."[18]

The desire for life is a desire for a fulfilling relationship, and the response to the desire for life is no more than a potentiality for relationship. The emergence of the signifier in the Other's space makes the potentiality to respond to the desire specific, makes it a *rational principle* – the signifier is the radical primary fact of the rational principle. But at the same time the rational character of the signifier also makes the desire specific as a rational demand for relationship. What the signifier signifies, what it "says" as it arises, is a signified potentiality for a fulfilling relationship, that is, for the fullness of life. And the signified potentiality has a specific reference – it is a principle corresponding to the subject's primary desire, a reciprocity of reference which turns the desire into the principle-rational demand. This referential reciprocity is the basis of the subject. It constitutes the subject as an existential fact of relationship, that is to say, as a rational existence: Existence possessing reason-rationality-language and capable of fitting into the language-rationality of natural order and human communion that existed before the subject.

The first signifier could be the mother's breast since the vital relationship connected with the primary desire is not abstract, but one of partaking of food, a real relationship which is a prerequisite of life. But the receiving of food does not exhaust desire, since the signified of food is the fulfilling relationship, that is, the fullness of life rather than biological survival. "If the provision of food is not combined with the experience of a presence, which doesn't cease to be signified whether present or lost, if desire's Other is not mediated by the supplier of the food's alternating presence and absence, the infant will never be introduced into the world of human beings, the world of language and symbols."[19]

Thus the vital and decisive question about the institution and formation of subjective existence concerns not the first signifier but what is ultimately signified, towards which the primary desire for fulfilling relationship (that is, for fulfilling life) turns, for ever unfulfilled. The desire's signifier always emerges in the space of the Other and this emergence institutes and consolidates the subject. The Other, however, always remains with a capital "O," is always the supreme goal of the fulfilling relationship, that is to say, of immortal life.

In the course of ephemeral individual life, the Other is "mediated" by the mother's breast, the presence-absence of the mother, food, caresses, the language of communication, the intervention of the image of the father – an intervention which "socializes" the vital relationship with the mother and forms the awareness of the ego as an autonomous third. The Other is "mediated" in maturity by the body in sexual union, by the astonishment of the familiar otherness of one's own children – an astonishment which releases embodiedness from the individuality of space-time. The Other is even "mediated" in a variety of ways by the authority of the law, the erotic beauty of nature, the infinite dynamics of the signifiers of art.

The subject is structured as an existential fact only by the vital reference to the presence-absence of the Other. A presence-absence which is signified as the goal of desire, without the signified ever being exhausted by the signifier of the longing, by the mediating principles which correspond to the radically primary and always unfulfilled desire.

If this is one positive approach to the human subject as an existential fact (besides the manifestly incomplete phenomenological or intellectualist-abstract definitions of the subject in its biological individuality), then whether the human person can exist in the mode of relation rather than in the mode of nature is not a problem. Because positive experiential analysis itself gives the question an affirmative answer.

At the same time, however, we cannot confirm the existence of the subjective factor in the mode of relationship experientially without presupposing a biologically given nature and a natural energy which acts as the foundation of the relation. Even the radically primary desire of the subject is operated in a "mediating" fashion by the subject's nature – its natural energies. And upon death it is nature which dies and every natural energy "is extinguished" in its entirety. Even if the mode of the relation is the only possibility for the subject to be established as an existential fact, it is manifested independently of the mode of nature and the subject's liability to death. It is manifested by the desire for fulfillment, that is, for immortal life.

Two contradictory affirmations, both equally confirmed by experience: the nature which undergirds and clearly limits – in terms of time and place – the exercise of the relationship; and the relation which institutes and forms the subject as an existential fact, always – in spite of nature's limitations – in the "field" of the transcendent Other's existence. In the "field" of the signified potentiality for "immortal life, a life which is unconstricted, which has no need of any organ, a life which has been simplified and made indissoluble."

The negation of one of subjectivity's two experiential givens would have arbitrarily curtailed experiential knowledge itself. It would have been a kind of cognitive suicide – with resorting to ideology as the inevitable result. We have positive knowledge of the subject only as something that operates through ephemeral natural operations and functions. But we also know it positively, only as a rational response of desire to the invitation of the transcendent Other, an invitation to a fulfilling relation, that is, to immortal life.

There appears to be only one way of resolving the impasse presented by these contradictory assertions: The study of the *rational referentiality* of every instance of that which exists. A study, drawing on real experience, of the reciprocity which is suggested by the rational reference, a study that points us to a *rational invitation* – a causal principle of the existential fact of all that is, of both nature and relation. The radical primary referentiality of the rational structuring of matter – as suggested by quantum physics – and the radical primary referentiality of the desire which forms the subject into a rational existence, both point to a unified rational invitation which institutes being in its fullness. They point to the "field" of the transcendent Other.

If the "anthropic principle" of contemporary physics functions as a methodological aid to research, why should the principle of the transcendent Other not function as a methodological aid to establishing a non-intellectualist, critically empirical ontology? The transcendent aspect of human *consciousness* in the strong form of the "anthropic principle" is the only solution to the otherwise perplexing "measurement problem" of quantum physics – a problem of structuring the information about the quantum wave as an existential fact of physical reality. Conversely, without recourse to the transcendent Other's *rational invitation*, without the principle of rational reciprocity, both the primary referentiality of the rational structuring of matter and the primary referentiality which establishes the human subject remain unexplained.

The ontological problem could not even be posited without the possibility of *rational* reference of the mode of nature and the mode of relation to the "field," that is, to the *invitation*, of the transcendent Other. The world's matter-energy and the human subject-person, as ontological givens, would remain uninterpretable. The problem of the *meaning* of human existence and of human action, of the world and of history (attributing meaning to mode of life, that is, to culture) would remain trapped in contradiction – a contradiction between two empirically validated and existent mutually exclusive givens: finite nature and infinite relation.

The psychoanalytical insistence on experiencing the referential formation of the subject, of the genesis of the subject in the field of the Other, together with the adherence of quantum physics to the radical primary referentiality and rational formation of matter, are elements of modernity's difficulty in constructing a postmodern metaphysics. The way forward lies fundamentally in a release both from the Newtonian phenomenology of that which exists and its concomitant intellectualist metaphysics, and from the Kantian "denial"[20] of metaphysics and its identification only with the analysis of the mind's cognitive function – trapping ontology in the nihilism or irrationality of "randomness."

The most fertile approach lies in demonstrating how the radical primary referentiality of what exists is rational-referential. Both the tracing back to the initial givens of the quantum formation of matter, and the analysis of how the subject originally emerged make us include a primary rational referentiality which institutes and forms what exists – a rational referentiality which can be defined only as a semantic correspondence to a signified rational invitation.

Modernity's legacy to the postmodern ontological problem is the empirically tested release of reasoning from being restricted to the rationality of the structure of the existent, and to the understanding of this structure as an evolved brain function. The more fruitful contribution of modernity to ontology is the interpretation of reason's presence as always the expression of a rational reciprocity – the presupposed reciprocity of the reference institutes and forms rationality.

Consequently modernity's legacy guides postmodern metaphysics to an interpretation of *being* as a rational reciprocity of relations: an interpretation which releases *being* from the *onticity* of Newtonian phenomenology and intellectualism, and releases the *subject* from the *discrete individuality* of materialist biology. In both cases, the referentiality of the reason-mode of existents refers to the hermeneutic attempt at an institutive rational invitation to relationship – the vital contribution of modernity to ontology is the capital "O" in the Other. More specifically, the study of the institution and structuring of the subject – a study of the referential reciprocity of desire and signifier, and also of the experiential distance between signifier and signified in the fulfilling reciprocity – points to the real difference between the mediating *others* and the *Other* which is the goal: the differentiation of existent things from authentic existence, of survival from life – ultimately of the created from the uncreated. Here we might add that the structure of the primary referentiality as a signifying rationality presupposes, in respect of its genesis, not the given presence of the Other but is presence-absence. Even the mediators in the primary reference constitute rational signifiers and render the reference rational only on the presupposition of their presence-absence. If the presence of the mother were given, constant and possessed by the infant, the signifier of desire in the field of the mother would not emerge, and consequently neither would the institution and structuring of the rational subject. If the Other of the presupposed rational invitation to relationship and of the desired aim of the relationship were a given and definite Newtonian presence, the emergence of signifiers of invitation and relationship would have been impossible, the rational existence of humanity would not have come into being. The real distance between physical and metaphysical, the freedom of the Other from subordination to definite certainties, is an existential presupposition of the rational subject.

If it is the invitation of the uncreated which constitutes the created, if it is the invitation of the Other which constitutes nature and subjectivity with the mode of relationship – with the longing response of the subject to the life-giving relationship mediated by nature – then why should this very invitation not transcend the mediation of nature and (still in the relational mode) consolidate subjectivity as an existential fact free from death?

The question leads us at least to control the consistency of linguistic semantics – that is, the presuppositions of rational consistency with experience – in the case of the only ontological proposition which attempts to give some meaning to the possibilities of the existence of the subject after death.

Thesis 3

A Postmodern Essay In Metaphysical Ontology

By the word *nature* I mean existential uniformity. Nature is the sum total of the reality of the cosmos, because it has createdness as the common form of its existence. I call "created" every existing thing which does not owe its existence to itself, which is not identical with its causal principle.

Nature is also the common form of existence in all the specific existents of the same kind: the sum total of the characteristics-properties-functions which constitute a common morphology of mode of existence. In this instance I identify the semantic content of the word *nature* with what is signified by the word *essence*. As a derivation from the infinitive of the Latin verb *esse* ("to be"), essence expresses the common morphology of some existents participating in existence.

By the word *hypostasis* I mean every specific existential realization of a common nature: any individual existence which draws together all the characteristics of a single species, always, however, in a unique manner compared with other hypostases of the same nature. The common characteristics of the natural species operate in every hypostasis in a form which is unique and distinct.

I call nature's *energies* the modes or functions which express both the existential uniformity of nature and the existential uniqueness of the hypostasis. We know nature only as existential energies, as a sum total of functions which constitute a common morphology of the mode of existence. And we know the hypostasis only as an energetic-existential otherness expressive of nature's common functions.

Without the reference to *energies*, the signifiers *nature* and *hypostasis* are exhausted in merely phenomenological significations. As a result of the distinction between nature and the hypostatically expressed energies of nature, the definition of the existential fact preserves the clarity of experiential proof.

The hypostasis of humanity is every individual human existence, every specific human being. The human hypostasis sums up the universal existential uniformity of human nature, the totality of the energies by which human nature is expressed and distinguished from every other natural species. The single hypostasis sums up the human whole's existential characteristics and existential powers – the bodily and psychological functions or capacities which make a human being an existential fact.

The existential summing up of human nature as a whole in a single human hypostasis is a unique, distinct and unrepeatable fact of existence. This otherness of the human hypostasis is not exhausted by the morphology of uniqueness. It also includes the dynamics of the unexpected, of the non-predetermined expression of the energies' operations, of the genuinely new and unprecedented. It is an active-creative otherness which is due to the existential power – of the human person alone – to set itself apart in its existence from the uniformity of nature, to activate some common natural energies with a distinctiveness which is not only morphological but belongs to an existential mode.

I call human *freedom* the power of modal distinctiveness, of existential-creative otherness with regard to common nature's uniformity. A limited but empirically proven power of the existential self-determination of the hypostasis, for a relative release from having to conform to the existential preconditions imposed by natural uniformity.

Once we accept the freedom (even if limited and relative)

of the existential self-determination of the hypostasis with regard to nature as an empirical fact, nature is proved to be "something more" or "something different" simply from the existential mode's morphological uniformity. Human nature is revealed as an autonomous existential fact within the limits of the existential fact of the hypostasis: as a tendency towards autonomy and existential priority of the commonly given function-needs of natural uniformity in the face of hypostatic otherness.

To experience nature as existential autonomy within the limits of the hypostasis is to experience a contradictory force with regard to hypostatic otherness, to experience an undifferentiated drive, impulse or instinct which militates against the existential distinctiveness of the hypostasis. The hypostasis tends to come into existence as otherness and freedom from nature, nature tending to subordinate the hypostasis to its uniform preconditions.

In this existential antithesis between human nature and hypostasis, the hypostasis prevails temporarily, but the final and irreversible victory goes to nature. Nature binds the hypostasis, since it is nature that provides the energies with which the hypostasis hypostasizes its existential otherness. And the energies of nature are of necessity subject to progressive decay or to unforeseen dysfunction-infirmity and, finally, to their "extinction" upon death.

Upon death the physical individuality, the psychosomatic reality of the individual human being disappears. The physical energies-powers which are hypostasized in the existential fact of individuality are obliterated: movement, thought, reason, judgment, imagination, memory, the senses, suffering, creativity – every natural energy.

For as long as natural individuality exists it hypostasizes dynamically, by free choice, the natural operation of perpetuating the species, the creation of progeny. The hypostasis proves to be effectively capable of perpetuating nature, while nature is proved to be incapable in practice of perpetuating the specific – the unique, distinctive and unrepeatable – hypostasis.

The only hint of freedom from natural necessity is the existential otherness of the hypostasis – or at least the temporary existential apartness of the hypostasis from nature. By studying, with the help of quantum physics, the existential distinctness of human consciousness from every natural system or, with the help of psychology-psychoanalysis, the existential distinctness of the human subject from biological individuality, we locate the hint of freedom from natural necessity in the fact of relationship. Consciousness and the subject are two relationship signifiers which refer to active otherness as existential identity and non-predetermined response to an invitation-to-relationship.

Consciousness and the subject are signifiers released from the limitation of reference restricted to mental referents only through the experience of relationship. I describe as *rational* a relation which is conscious and free, because it is effected by the natural power of reason. It is not, however, rationality (nor is it consciousness or the subject) which institutes the existential fact of relation. Relation forms reason; reason does not form relation. Relation also forms the subject, the consciousness and the unconscious of the subject.[1]

Relation is what underlies (is the *sub-jectum* of) rationality and conscious existence: it is the starting point and presupposition of an existential and conscious freedom from nature; it is the *sub-jectum* of the hypostatic response to an "ontopoeic"[2] – generative of existential identity – invitation.

Relationship is not an epiphenomenon of the subject's existence, but a presupposition for the institution and formation of the subject as an existential fact. This existential fact, instituted and formed only through relation, only as a referential response to a pre-existing invitation-to-relationship, expresses its reference in its mode of nature: the natural activity of desire and of reason. But the natural expression of the referentiality points to a pre-natural factor of referentiality – to a "nucleus" (*Kern*, as Freud called it) derived from non-sense[3], that is, from something that transcends all meaning, which is meaning's hypostatic potentiality, the initial potentiality of the referentiality of the subject. The subject is instituted and formed as an existential factor of referential reciprocity, as a term of a relation.

The only existential fact which may, as an empirical given, be discerned as differentiated from the existential fact of nature, is the *relation*. And if nature is the existential uniformity of the created (as we saw at the beginning), then the difference or "distance" of the *relation* from *nature* may be declarative of, or simply referential to, the existential mode that is neither subject to nature nor expressed by nature, that is, the mode of existence of the uncreated. Then the subject, as a hypostatic response to a presupposed reciprocity of pre-natural relation, owes its institutive initial impulse to the invitatory activity of the uncreated. The subject is generated in the "space" of the transcendent Other.

If the experience of relation refers, at least indirectly and incompletely, to the mode of existence of the uncreated, if the only possibility of semantic access to the uncreated is the experience of relation, then the linguistic signifiers which can express the uncreated Causal Principle of the created as an existential fact of relation are also the signifiers of the *One* and *Trihypostatic Principle*.

The attribution of arithmetic *unicity* to the Causal Principle does not refer to a definition of essence or nature. For the definition of essence or nature signifies the existential fact's given presuppositions which are excluded when we speak of a *Causal Principle* – a Principle which is antecedent to every existential definition. The unicity of the Causal Principle cannot signify, in the experiential rudiments of the semantics of a language, anything but the freedom of a will-to-existence unfettered by any natural-essential presupposition. And the existential potentiality of this will-to-existence is structured as a hypostatic fact of relation, that is, of a non-presupposed existential freedom of hypostases that participate in being.

In our experiential model of a semantics of human language, only a will-to-existence unfettered by any natural-essential presupposition or intentionality can be an absolutely non-self-interested *love*. Only love, as an ontological (rather than an ethical) category, can express self-transcendence and self-offering – a communion with being – as a volitional mode of existence: only love can refer to an existence which exists not through necessarily acquiescing to the fact of its existence, but through freely hypostasizing its being (by coming forth as distinct hypostases of its being) – producing hypostases by "generation" and "procession" with which it structures being as a communion of love.

The volitional-loving distinction of hypostases is the only way in which we can signify linguistically the Causal Principle of what exists as an existential fact of relation free from any antecedent definition. Whether blind necessity or freedom is the causal principle of what exists, the possibility of freedom has only a single ontological precedent: the one referring to a volitional distinction of Hypostases of the One Causal Principle. The distinction of hypostases which structure being as a communion of love is the only semantic formulation capable of indicating experientially a single, always unified but not unitary, will-to-existence which is existentially self-confirming as a fact of freedom.

With the experiential model of the semantics of human language, the initial hypostatic realization of being as a communion of love can only be *triadic*: we recognize the relation which forms the subject as a discrete hypostasis only as a non-dualistic one, that is, as non-dependence on the institutive principle. If the third does not arise in the "space" of the Other, the radically primary referentiality of the subject will never constitute a relation – freedom from dependence on duality will never be established.

I use the term *person* to define existence as a fact of relation: the epistemically immediate awareness of freedom which makes relations possible, the otherness of the existential realization of relations which emerges from the freedom of the relation. Epistemic immediacy signifies a self-defined existential referentiality, that is, the immediate awareness of freedom and the rationality of reference. An existence capable of realizing the relation's existential freedom, of communing with being, of loving and being loved, is an existence which is "self-aware" and rational, an existence which is productive of non-predetermined expressions of its reason.

I also define the human subject as a *personal* existence, even though it expresses its relation existentially with the modes-energies of nature's limitations. Self-awareness, rationality, the power to create, active existential otherness, are also characteristics of the human subject, but dependent on the limitations of created nature. Nevertheless, I also define the human subject as *personal* existence, since the relation's natural expression refers experientially to a pre-natural factor of referentiality: to the relation's "nucleus" or hypostatic term, which is presupposed by the reference's real-existential character, and which defines itself existentially only by the mode of relation.

If the human subject is the hypostatic response to a pre-natural invitation-to-relationship, if it owes its existential inception to the invitatory energy of the uncreated, then its *personal* character lies in its freedom to constitute or to reject existence as a reciprocal relationship, as a loving communion with being.

The human person expresses the relationship with the modes-energies of nature existentially. If this existential expression constitutes a free denial of the reciprocity of love (of the mode by which the uncreated constitutes existence), then the extinction of natural energies upon death must also be the definitive end of the subject's existence. If, however, the existential expression of the subject's relationship with its uncreated institutive principle constitutes a free affirmation of love's reciprocity, then what are the modes-energies, what is the nature, with which love's affirmation can be expressed after biological death? What can created humanity's personal hypostasis hypostasize when the energies of its created being have been extinguished?

If nature is created and neither inexplicably eternal nor irrationally random, if what exists has an uncreated Causal Principle, then we must distinguish uncreated energies of the Causal Principle, which express outside time the triadic existential fact of a communion of hypostases; and the created results of these same uncreated energies which constitute the world's reality, or nature.

(The signifier "uncreated" refers to existence that is not subject to creation and is consequently free from every limitation of beginning, or inception and end. The signifier "created" refers to existence that is not responsible for its own being, and consequently is subject to beginning, or inception and possible end.)

The natural energies by which the human subject's personal hypostasis is expressed existentially are plainly created and are extinguished upon death. But even the hypostatic "nucleus" which constitutes the subject as an existential term of the presupposed reciprocity of a pre-natural relation is also created. The difference between these two created givens lies in the *personal* potentialities of the hypostatic "nucleus" for subjectivity: Potentialities by which it can express existentially (through the created energies which it hypostasizes) an acceptance or refusal of the pre-natural invitation-to-relationship which constitute it. Acceptance or refusal of the loving mode of existence of the uncreated.

Along with the experiential model of human language, only

by referring to the uncreated's energies can we adumbrate humankind's possible existence after death with an ontological implication – energies offered as "grace" so that the human subject can hypostasize them as a *personal* existential fact. Such an interpretation constitutes a "proposition that has sense:" That is, it "determines a place in logical space" and "the whole of logical space must already be given by it."[4]

The above proposition regulates the whole logical space of the coordinates which constitute it. This does not mean that it explains the origin of the constituent elements in an apodictic manner. Rather, it *shows* its sense[5] by arranging the constituent elements in a comprehensible and coherent order. The adumbrated elements are as follows:

(i) If there exists an uncreated Causal Principle for what exists, it exists only in the mode of loving self-transcendence and self-offering.

(ii) If there exists a human subject, it exists only as a result of the invitatory energy of the uncreated, which is only loving.

(iii) If the invitation-to-relationship is only loving and if the existential response to the invitation is affirmation, then the hypostasization of the uncreated invitatory energies by the invitation's created recipient is the only possible purpose (goal) of the invitatory energy.

Is it, however, conceptually coherent for the created to hypostasize the uncreated? The reply's logical place (experiential expression) may be located only in the definitive coordinates which are presupposed by the signifier *energies*: The energies express the existential fact without being identified with the "essential" or hypostatic otherness of what expresses them.

We draw semantic adumbrations from the experience of the created, and with the data of this experience we recognize that Mozart's music expresses the subject's (Mozart's) hypostatic otherness, without identifying the music with the essential or hypostatic otherness of the subject, which is Mozart. The music "is shared indivisibly by all in the same way that one and the same sound is perceived by all,"[6] without this participation producing divisions in the hypostatic subject that has produced the musical energy, and without making the participants in the effect also participants in the hypostatic otherness of the producer.

The subject is generated always and necessarily in the "space" of the transcendent Other. If the radically primary referentiality of the subject (as an existential-hypostatic response to a pre-natural invitation-to-relationship) hypostasizes the desire's natural energy, then even the possibility of the subject's rebirth after death (a possibility that it should hypostasize uncreated energies of the inviting transcendent Other) does not violate the logical space of the original proposition. And as always the rational form of the proposition refers to conceivable signifieds which the logical form itself as an indication never exhausts.

If the human subject exists as a result of the invitatory energy of the uncreated, which is only loving, and if the existential response to the invitation is not an acceptance, but a refusal, then we may draw one of two possible conclusions: Either the voluntary refusal of the created destroys and invalidates the voluntary loving energy of the uncreated, or the voluntary loving energy of the uncreated, which is timeless, also renders the existential refusal of the created timeless. The first possibility destroys the logical space of what is signified by the uncreated. The second does not.

The possibility that we should exist after death, even when our existential response to the invitation of the uncreated is a refusal, is signified in religious language by the word "hell," which in Greek is *kolasis*. The primary meaning of the Greek word is truncation, trimming down, curtailment. The secondary meaning is corrective punishment, torment.

The proposition-with-sense which may be constructed

from both senses of the Greek word for "hell" refers to the absolute character of a love which steadfastly respects freedom, even when freedom hypostasizes the refusal of a loving reciprocity. In that event, the trimming down-truncation-curtailment of the existential possibilities (possibilities of *being* as a loving relationship) arises not from a deficiency of "grace" or the offer of life-giving energy, but from the free refusal of grace's recipient to hypostasize it as an existential fact of relationship. In that event, too, "hell" is only a voluntary self-punishment, the torment of an existence which actively destroys itself without being able to nullify its hypostatic structure.

If the coordinates of the above semantic analysis form the logical space of the signifier "hell" (if the invitation of the uncreated constituting the subject is only and absolutely loving, and if freedom is not ephemeral and natural, but the institutive and unalterable characteristic of the subject's *personal* existence), then the definition of immutability (the unalterable) does not belong to the logical space which is defined by the signifier "hell."

Philosophical ontology cannot be anything more than a critique of the coherence presented by the semantics of language in adumbrating the existential fact. Coherence is judged not by intellectualist-methodological criteria but by criteria which are significative-experiential: If the linguistic propositions are propositions-with-sense, if they *show* their truth by referring to the experiential coordinates of intelligibility, one should be able to accept with this interpretation of critical coherence Wittgenstein's aphorism that: "All philosophy is a 'critique of language'."[7]

The semantics of the analysis of the possibility of metaphysics has not emerged historically from the primary theoretical questions which have been posed here. This linguistic semantics has been shaped as an expression and formulation of a specific historical experience. Historical experience is not controlled by theoretical analysis. It is verified or falsified only by a living participation in experience. Theoretical analysis controls exclusively the semantic expression and formulation of experience.

Consequently, the analytical path which I have followed here represents a retracing of the model of a cognitive approach to the possibility of metaphysics. This retracing is not superfluous or pointless. Often the cognitive approach to the possibility of metaphysics is made difficult or impossible by inconsistency in the linguistic semantics expressing the historical experience of the transcendent Other. The individualistic psychological demand for intellectual certainties and their utilitarian ideological exploitation invalidate the semantic coordinates of reference to experience, block the cognitive approach to the possibility of metaphysics with the suspicion of illusion.

The barrier to a cognitive approach to the possibility of metaphysics, a barrier formed by the fear of illusion, is what paralyzes the ontological quest in modernity. The removal of the barrier seems to be a necessary and attainable condition for entry into a postmodern "paradigm."

NOTES

Prolegomena 1

[1] A. Lalande, *Vocabulaire de la philosophie*, Paris: P.U.F. 1972, p. 640: "L' 'histoire moderne' est l'histoire des faits postérieurs à la prise de Constantinople, en 1453."

2 Herbert Butterfield, *The Origins of Modern Science 1300-1800*, London: Bell 1957, p. vii.

[3] For a fuller analysis of modernity's anti-religious polemic see the following studies of P. Kondyles: *Hê kritikê tês metaphysikês stê neôterê skepsê*, Athens: Gnosi 1983; *Ho Eurôpaikos Diaphôtismos*, 2 vols, Athens: Themelio 1987; *Hê parakmê tou Astikou Politismou*, Athens: Themelio 1991. In what follows I am much indebted to Kondyles.

[4] J. Robinson, *Economic Philosophy*, London: Watts 1962, p. 45.

[5] Cf. K.B. Krimbas, *Darvinika*, Athens: Ermes 1986: "We are so accustomed to our anthropocentric perspective ... that we find it very difficult to regard the living species around us as of equal value or to accept that our uniqueness as a biological species is not a compelling reason for our supremacy [...]. We do not dare contemplate that in a world that has evolved without a goal and usually without a route mapped out in advance, we are simultaneously both the spectators and the actors in an act accomplished without purpose, without meaning, without belief in the existence of any metaphysical safety valves. This is the world into which Charles Darwin brought us about 130 years ago."

[6] The "first truth" which emerges from the study of Nature is "perhaps humbling for humanity," since humanity is now part of the same series as the other animals: Comte de Buffon, *Histoire naturelle*, cited by Kondyles, *Ho Eurôpaikos Diaphôtismos*, vol. 1, p. 347.

[7] Cf. P. Kondyles, *Ho Eurôpaikos Diaphôtismos*, p. 348: "These ideas turn, naturally, against the theological understanding of man as made in the image and likeness of God, from which the paradox arises that the very theology that champions the dignity and the privileged status of man was also, from the perspective of modern rationalism, regarded from the beginning as supremely inimical to man and humiliating of him."

[8] *Tractatus Logico-Philosophicus* 3.262 (trans. D.F. Pears – B.F. McGuinness).

[9] See Louis Althusser, "Idéologie et appareils idéologiques d'Etat," in *La pensée*, June 1970, reprinted in *Positions*, Paris: Editions Sociales 1976.
[10] The classic analysis of the consumer attitude of modern people to art is Christopher Small, *Music, Society, Education*, London: Calder 1977.
[11] There is an analysis of ancient Greek political ideas in my books, *Schediasma Eisagôgês stê Philosophia*, 3rd edn, Athens: Domos 1990, sections 13 and 16, and *Orthos logos kai koinônikê praktikê*, 2nd edn, Athens: Domos 1990, V 1a.
[12] There is a discussion of the political appeal to the ecclesiastical model of participation in true life in my books, *Kephalaia politikês theologias*, 2nd edn, Athens: Kas. Grigori 1983, 5.6; *To keno stên trechousa politikê*, 2nd edn, Athens: Kastaniotes 1992, XIII; *To pragmatiko kai to phantasiôdes stên Politikê Oikonomia*, Athens: Domos 1989, 10 a-d.
[13] There is a discussion of the eudaemonistic values governing economics in my book, *To pragmatiko kai to phantasiôdes*, 4, together with the relevant bibliography.
[14] See U. Dierse, "Ideologie," in the *Historische Wörterbuch der Philosophie*, vol. 4, Schwabe-Verlag 1976, col. 158 ff, where there is a full bibliography.
[15] See Sigmund Freud, *Die Zukunft einer Illusion*, 1927 (ET: *The Future of an Illusion*, trans. W. D. Robson-Scott, 1928).
[16] See, for example, Jürgen Habermas, "Psychoanalyse und Gesellschaftstheorie," in his *Erkenntnis und Interesse* III, 12; Jean-François Lyotard, *Economie libidinale*, Paris: Minuit 1974; Gérard Mendel, *La psychanalyse revisitée*, Paris: La Découverte 1988; Gilles Lipovetsky, *L'empire de l'éphémère*, Paris: Gallimard 1987; Janine Chasseguet-Smirgel, "Quelques réflexions d'un psychanalyste sur l'idéologie," in *Pouvoirs* 11 (1981), pp. 33-40.

Prolegomena 2

[1] Classic examples in the relevant bibliography: Max Weber, *Wirtschaft und Gesellschaft*, Tübingen: Mohr 1976 (ET: *Economy and Society*, trans. E. Fischoff *et al.*, Berkeley: University of California Press 1979); Max Horkheimer – Theodor Adorno, *Dialektik der Aufklärung*, Frankfurt: Fischer 1969; Herbert Marcuse, *One-dimensional Man: Studies in the Ideology of Advanced Industrial Society*, 2nd ed, Boston, Mass.: Beacon Press 1991; Jürgen Habermas, *Theorie und Praxis*, Frankfurt am Main: Suhrkamp 1974 (ET: *Theory and Practise*, trans. John Viertal, Cambridge: Polity 1988); Hans Albert, *Freiheit und Ordnung*, Tübingen: Mohr 1986; Jean-François Lyotard, *Discours, figure*, Paris: Klincksieck 1971.

[2] The expression is that of Pierre Legendre, *Le désir politique de Dieu: Essai sur les montages de l'Etat et du Droit*, Paris: Fayard 1988, p. 221.
[3] Alain Badiou, *L'être et l'événement*, Paris: Seuil 1988.
[4] *One-dimensional Man*, pp. 2-4.
[5] See Small, *Music, Society, Education.*
[6] *Tractatus* 2.1512 (trans. Pears-McGuinness).
[7] *Tractatus* 6.13 (trans. Pears-McGuinness).
[8] *Tractatus* 4.12 (trans. Pears-McGuinness).
[9] *Tractatus* 6.41, 6.42, 6.421.
[10] *Tractatus* 4.003, 4.0031, 6.53.

Prolegomena 3

[1] See M.-D. Chenu, *La théologie comme science au XIIIe siècle*, Paris: Vrin 1969, p. 58ff.
[2] See further, my *Orthos logos kai koinônikê praktikê*, pp. 14-19, 185-210.
[3] See for example *The Works of Francis Bacon*, ed. J. Spedding, R.L. Ellis, and D.D. Heath, London: Longmans 1879, 3, 218; T. Hobbes, *Leviathan*, London 1651, 43, 449; I. Kant, *Kritik der Urteilskraft*, 91, *Logik* IX.
[4] *Tractatus* 6.41 (trans. Pears-McGuinness).
[5] *Tractatus* 6.52: "We feel that even if *all possible* scientific questions have been answered, the problems of life remain completely untouched. Of course there are then no questions left, and this itself is the answer." (trans. Pears-McGuinness).
[6] *Einführung in die Metaphysik*, Tübingen: Niemeyer 1958, p. 14.
[7] "C'est la libido, en tant que pur instinct de vie c'est-à-dire de vie immortelle, de vie irrépressible, de vie qui n'a besoin, elle, d'aucun organe, de vie simplifiée et indestructible:" Jacques Lacan, *Le séminaire* XI, Paris: Seuil 1973, p. 180.
[8] See the important discussion of P. Kondyles in his *Ho Eurôpaikos Diaphôtismos*, vol. 1, pp. 76, 425-6, and vol. 2, pp. 39-44, 69-86. See also Ch. Yannaras, *To pragmatiko kai to phantasiôdes*, chapter 8, section a.
[9] Cf. Julien de La Mettrie, *Anti-Sénèque ou Discours sur le Bonheur, Oeuvres philosophiques*, Berlin 1774, vol 2, pp. 89, 116, 130; Marquis de Sade, *Juliette* I-IV, *Oeuvres complètes*, Paris 1962-4, vol. 8, pp. 59-60, 201-2, 299; vol 9, pp. 107-8; P. Kondyles, *Ho Eurôpaïkos Diaphôtismos*, vol. 2, pp. 184-202.
[10] For further details see my *Schediasma Eisagôgês stê Philosophia*, section 5.
[11] See, for example, P. Kondyles, *Ho Eurôpaïkos Diaphôtismos*, vol. 1,

ch. 4.2.3; vol. 2, ch. 6.2; Karl Popper, *Die beiden Grundprobleme der Erkenntnistheorie*, Tübingen: Mohr 1979, vol. 1 ch. 4.44.

[12] See the detailed discussion in N. Nissiotis, *Prolegomena eis tên theologikên gnôsiologian*, Athens 1965, pp. 173-83; also: A. Farrer, *The Glass of Vision*, London 1948; Jacques Maritain, *Distinguer pour unir*, Paris 1935; Reinhold Niebuhr, *Essays in Applied Christianity*, New York 1959.

[13] See Kirk, Raven and Schofield, *The Presocratic Philosophers*, Cambridge: Cambridge University Press. 1983, p. 420: The Atomists emphasized the other side of unpremeditated mechanical processes, that is, necessity. Thus Leucippus, in his only extant saying, declares: "Nothing occurs at random, but everything for a reason and by necessity;" A.A. Long, *Hellenistic Philosophy*, London: Duckworth 1974, pp. 37-8, 40-1: "This swerve which atoms make at no determined time or place [...] builds into the universe, as Epicurus conceives of this, a principle of relative indeterminacy [...]. All of [the infinite number of worlds] are ultimately explicable by reference to the purposeless combination and separation of discrete and inanimate physical entities moving in empty space [...]. [I]t is necessary to remember that Epicurus did not set out to be a purely disinterested investigator of things. According to his own words, 'the purpose of studying nature is to gain a sharp understanding of the cause of those things which are most important' (*Ep. Hdt.* 78). By 'most important' he means fundamental to human well-being."

[14] "For the things which come-to-be by natural process all do so either always or for the most part in a given way; while any exceptions – any results which occur neither always nor for the most part – are products of chance and spontaneity" *On Generation and Corruption* 2.6, 333b 5-7 (trans. H.H. Joachim).

[15] "Things *do*, in a way, occur by chance, for they occur accidentally and chance is an accidental cause. But it is not the cause without qualification of anything." "These spontaneous events are said to be from chance if they have the further characteristics of being the objects of choice and happening to agents capable of choice." *Physics* 2.5, 197a 13-14; 2.6, 197b 20-2 (trans. R.P. Hardie and R.K. Gaye).

[16] See more fully my *Schediasma Eisagôgês stê Philosophia*, Section 27.

[17] M. Heidegger, *Nietzsche*, vol. 2, Pfullingen: Neske-Verlag 1961, p. 92; ibid., *Holzwege*, 4th ed, Frankfurt: Klostermann 1963, pp. 204, 239-40.

[18] Jacques Lacan, *Le séminaire* XI, p. 23; ibid., *Écrits*, vol. 2, Paris: Seuil 1971, p. 203.

Parenthesis 1

[1] "A proposition determines a place in logical space. The existence of this logical place is guaranteed by the mere existence of the constituents – by the existence of the proposition with a sense." "A proposition can determine only one place in logical space: nevertheless the whole of logical space must already be given by it." Wittgenstein, *Tractatus* 3.4, 3.42 (trans. Pears-McGuinness).
[2] "The sense of the world must lie outside the world. In the world everything is as it is, and everything happens as it does happen: *in* it no value exists – and if it did exist, it would have no value. If there is any value that does have value, it must lie outside the whole sphere of what happens and is the case. For all that happens and is the case is accidental. What makes it non-accidental cannot lie *within* the world, since if it did it would itself be accidental. It must lie outside the world." Wittgenstein, *Tractatus* 6.41 (trans. Pears-McGuinness).
[3] See Stephen Hawking, *A Brief History of Time*, London: Bantam Books 1988, ch. 8: "The Origin and Fate of the Universe."
[4] Wittgenstein, *Tractatus* 4.464.
[5] Wittgenstein, *Tractatus* 5.155 (trans. Pears-McGuinness).
[6] See E.N. Oikonomou, *Hê physikê sêmera*, Herakleion: University of Crete Publications 1990, vol. 1, pp. 170 and 190; Jacques Monod, *Le hasard et la nécessité*, ET: *Chance and Necessity* (trans. A. Wainhouse), London: Collins 1972, pp. 110-13.

Parenthesis 2

[1] "Darwin's theory has no more to do with philosophy than any other hypothesis in natural science." "Philosophy sets limits to the much disputed sphere of natural science." Wittgenstein, *Tractatus* 4.1122, 4.113 (trans. Pears-McGuinness).
[2] See Parenthesis 1, No.1.
[3] "This fundamental concept of *gratuity* – i.e., the independence, chemically speaking, between the function itself and the nature of the chemical signals controlling it – applies to allosteric enzymes. In this case one and the same protein molecule does double duty as a specific catalyst and as a transducer of chemical signals [...]. Between the substrate of an allosteric enzyme and the ligands prompting or inhibiting its activity there exists no *chemically necessary* relationship of structure or of reactivity [...]. In short, the very *gratuitousness* of these systems, giving molecular evolution a practically limitless field for exploration and experiment, enabled it to elaborate the huge network of cybernetic interconnections

which makes each organism an autonomous functional unit, whose performances appear to transcend, if not to escape, the laws of chemistry." Monod, *Chance and Necessity*, pp. 78-9 (trans. A. Wainhouse).

[4] Cornelius Castoriadis, *Les carrefours du labyrinthe*, ET: *Crossroads in the Labyrinth* (trans. K. Soper and M.H. Ryle, modified), Brighton: Harvester Press, pp. 185-6; see also Monod, *Chance and Necessity*, p. 136: "The biosphere looks like the product of a unique event .... Among all the events possible in the universe the *a priori* probability of any particular one of them occurring is next to zero."

[5] Castoriadis, *Crossroads*, p. 186 (trans. Soper-Ryle, modified); There are recent indications that the law of entropy is valid for the universe as a whole (which is a "closed" system) but is not valid for the cell (which is an "open" system, exchanging matter and energy with the environment). Consequently, we have here two different forms of the behavior of matter, not the violation of the laws of its behavior . The supplying of the earth's biosphere with external matter and energy creates a negative entropy which is not at all incompatible with the laws of nature. Thus the question of randomness is transferred to the self-organizing "capacity" of matter when some external cause (the sun's rays) disturbs the chemical balance. How "random" is such a self-organizing activity, which although compatible with the laws of nature manifests a very high probability of non-conformity? See I. Prigogine and I. Stengers, *Order out of Chaos: Man's New Dialogue with Nature*, London: Flamingo 1985; W.J. Moore, *Physical Chemistry*, London: Longman 1972.

[6] Castoriadis, *Crossroads*, pp. 185-6 (trans. Soper-Ryle, modified).

[7] "The present structure of the biosphere certainly does not exclude the possibility that the decisive event occurred *only once*. Which would mean that its *a priori* probability was virtually zero." Monod, *Chance and Necessity* (trans. Wainhouse), p. 136.

[8] "To be more specific: these structures are 'random' in the sense that, even knowing the exact order of 199 residues in a protein containing 200, it would be impossible to formulate any rule, theoretical or empirical, enabling us to predict the nature of the one residue not yet identified by analysis." Monod, *Chance and Necessity*, p. 95 (trans. Wainhouse).

[9] See K. Popper, *Die Logik der Forschung*, Tübingen: Mohr 1976, pp. 3, 17, 72-3, ET: *The Logic of Scientific Discovery*, London: Routledge 1992; Imre Lacatos, "Changes in the Problem of Inductive Logic," in *The Problem of Inductive Logic*, Amsterdam: North Holland Publishing Co. 1988, pp. 315-417.

[10] Monod, *Chance and Necessity*, p. 117 (trans. Wainhouse).

[11] Wittgenstein, *Tractatus* 4.461 (trans. Pears-McGuinness).

[12] Monod, *Chance and Necessity*, pp. 137-8 (trans. Wainhouse).

[13] Monod, *Chance and Necessity*, pp. 138-9 (trans. Wainhouse).
[14] Monod, *Chance and Necessity*, p. 138 (trans. Wainhouse).
[15] Monod, *Chance and Necessity*, p. 139 (trans. Wainhouse).
[16] Monod, *Chance and Necessity*, p. 123 (trans. Wainhouse).
[17] See, for example: John Eccles, *Facing Reality*, Basel: Editions Roche-Springer 1973, chapters 4, 5 and 8; Karl Popper and John Eccles, *Das Ich und sein Gehirn*, Munich-Zurich: Piper-Verlag 1982, chapters E7 and E8.
[18] Monod, *Chance and Necessity*, p. 139.
[19] See "pulsion" in J. Laplanche and J.-B. Pontalis, *Vocabulaire de la psychanalyse*, 7th ed, Paris: P.U.F. 1981, p. 359 ff.
[20] Cornelius Castoriadis, *L'institution imaginaire de la société*, Paris: Seuil 1975.
[21] Jean-Paul Sartre, *L'etre et le néant*, Paris: Gallimard 1943, p. 124.
[22] Castoriadis, *Crossroads*, p. 200 (trans. Soper-Ryle).

Thesis 1

[1] For the etymological derivation and evolution of the semantic use of the term "apophaticism," see my *Orthos logos kai koinônikê praktikê*, 2nd ed, Athens: Domos 1990, 5.1.
[2] Richard Feynman (Nobel prize winner for physics 1965), *QED: The Strange Theory of Light and Matter*, Princeton: Princeton University Press 1985 pp. 19, 77.
[3] Alastair Rae (professor of theoretical physics at the University of Birmingham), *Quantum Physics: Illusion or Reality*? Cambridge: Cambridge University Press 1986, p. 110.
[4] Hawking, *Brief History of Time*, p. 61.
[5] Rae, *Quantum Physics*, p. 28; P. Coveney and R. Highfield, *The Arrow of Time*, London: W.H. Allen 1990; Paul Davies, *God and the New Physics*, London: J.M. Dent 1983. A quantum wave extended in space and containing, according to probability theory, the two properties of the system (particle-wave), "contracts" instantaneously at the moment of its observation and – depending on the method and the apparatus – one of the two properties constituting its physical existence disappears. This means that all the remaining points in space, however distant they may be, "inform" the fact of the observation and nullify the probability of the appearance of the second property of the system. That is to say, the mutual influence of separated states when there is no known interaction between them is confirmed.
[6] Rae, *Quantum Physics*, p. 93; Hawking, *Brief History of Time*, p. 65.
[7] Oikonomou, *Physikê sêmera*, vol. 1, p. 161; see also Jonathan Powers,

Philosophy and the New Physics, London and New York: Methuen 1982, p. 130 ff.
[8] Feynman, *QED*, p. 85.
[9] Feynman, *QED*, p. 95.
[10] If the charge constitutes the real identity of the electron, the mode in which the electron exists – since the electron is defined as the smallest possible elementary particle with a negative electrical charge – then the change of the charge is accompanied by a change of identity, which implies a new ontological reality.
[11] Rae, *Quantum Physics*, p. 42.
[12] Rae, *Quantum Physics*, p. 107.
[13] Oikonomou, *Physikê sêmera*, vol. 1, pp. 4 and 213.
[14] Cf. Richard Feynman in Paul Davies (ed.), *Superstrings: A Theory of Everything*, Cambridge: Cambridge University Press 1988, p. 204.
[15] Castoriadis, *Crossroads*, pp. 181-2 (trans. Soper-Ryle).
[16] Manolis Sarres, "Scholia stis kosmologikes kai physikes theôries tou mikrokosmou," *Synaxis* 18 (1986), p. 57.
[17] Rae, *Quantum Physics*, p. 9. It should be noted that of the two theories that make up the contemporary revolution in physics (relativity and quantum mechanics), the former modified and expanded classic mechanics while respecting the prevailing laws. By accepting, however, the immutability of the speed of light, it arrived at conclusions which contradicted Newtonian physics. Quantum theory, by contrast, overturned the prevailing laws, abolished a mechanistic understanding of causality (on the level of the microcosm), and provoked scientific and philosophical controversy. In spite of the fact that the Special Theory of Relativity (alone) was incorporated into the theories of anti-matter and the quantum field, the basic difference between the two systems remains. Nevertheless, with regard to "apophatic" language, and "unorthodox" methodology, both relativity and quantum mechanics converge in a striking way: They introduce ideas which challenge our representational way of thinking and describe the world in a manner which transcends the logic of our certainties on the macroscopic level.
[18] Oikonomou, *Physikê sêmera*, vol. 1, p. 193.
[19] Rae, *Quantum Physics*, p. 3.
[20] Hawking, *Brief History of Time*, p. 38.
[21] Oikonomou, *Physikê sêmera*, vol. 1, pp. 174 and 191.
[22] Oikonomou, *Physikê sêmera*, vol. 1, p. 190.
[23] Hawking, *Brief History of Time*, pp. 61, 62.
[24] Eyvind Wichmann, *Quantum Physics*, vol. 4 of *Berkeley Physics Course*, New York: McGraw-Hill 1971, pp. 50-60.
[25] See John Schwarz, in Davies, *Superstrings*, pp. 120, 133; Richard

Feynman in Davies, *Superstrings*, pp. 207-8.
[26] *Physics* 4.4, 212a15-16 and 20-21; 4.2, 209b1-2; *On the Heavens* 4.3, 310b7-8. There is a fuller discussion of these Aristotelian themes in my *Schediasma Eisagôgês*, section 31.
[27] *Frgm*. 91, ed. Diels-Kranz, I, 171.9.
[28] Discussions of the theme on a popular level in Hawking, *Brief History of Time*, ch. 2; Jayant Narlikar, *The Lighter Side of Gravity*, New York: Freeman 1982, ch. 5; Davies, *God and the New Physics*, ch. 9.
[29] See Hawking, *Brief History of Time*, p. 31; Oikonomou, *Physikê sêmera*, vol. 1, pp. 76-8, 126 ff. Cf. Davies, *God and the New Physics*; Narlikar, *The Lighter Side of Gravity*.
[30] Oikonomou, *Physikê sêmera*, vol. 1, p. 139. Cf. Narlikar, *The Lighter Side of Gravity*.
[31] For further details see Hawking, *Brief History of Time*, pp. 36-7.
[32] Besides, "light is in constant interaction with matter, without the power to escape from it, to come directly to us:" Vasileios Xanthopoulos, *Peri asterôn kai sympantôn*, Herakleion: University of Crete Publications 1991, p. 85.
[33] Xanthopoulos, *Peri asterôn*, p. 78.
[34] Stephanos Trachanas, "Tychê ê anagkaiotêta?" in Oikonomou, *Physikê sêmera*, vol. 2, pp. 386-7.
[35] Trachanas, "Tychê ê anagkaiotêta?", p. 392.
[36] Trachanas, "Tychê ê anagkaiotêta?", p. 406.
[37] Xanthopoulos, *Peri asterôn*, p. 81.
[38] Hawking, *Brief History of Time*, p. 160.
[39] Feynman, *QED*, p. 98.
[40] The word "quality" was introduced into the vocabulary of contemporary physics by Freeman Dyson ("Energy in the Universe," in *Scientific American* 225/3 (1971), pp. 50-9). It defines a localized energy capable of producing work with ordered movement. When the energy is dispersed (usually in the form of heat) what is dissolved is its *quality*, not its quantity. The qualitative aspect of the localized energy, on the basis of the work produced (the actual result) is most fully expressed and "represented" in the hermeneutic proposition of the *theory of superstrings*. This theory tells us that the elementary forms of matter are units of energy and the most elementary manifestations of energy are disturbances in the quantum field which may be described as the vibration of strings. See the discussions by Edward Witten, John Ellis and John Schwartz in Paul Davies (ed.), *Superstrings*.
[41] An expression borrowed from the *Corpus Dionysiacum* of the 5th century AD: *On the Divine Names* 9, Migne, PG 3, 825A.
[42] From the Foreword to John D. Barrow and Frank J. Tipler, *The An-*

thropic Cosmological Principle, Oxford: Oxford University Press 1988, p. vii.

[43] Hawking, *Brief History of Time*, p. 138.

[44] Xanthopoulos, *Peri asterôn*, p. 115; Hawking, *Brief History of Time*, pp. 137-8, 201; Barrow and Tipler, *Anthropic Cosmological Principle*, pp. 28 ff, 497ff, 556ff; Trachanas, "Tychê ê anagkaiotêta?," p. 386.

[45] Trachanas, "Tychê ê anagkaiotêta?," pp. 415-16; Barrow and Tipler, *Anthropic Cosmological Principle*, pp. 4-6.

[46] Hawking, *Brief History of Time*, p. 138.

[47] Rae, *Quantum Physics*, p. 67; Barrow and Tipler, *Anthropic Cosmological Principle*, p. 503; Trachanas, "Tychê ê anagkaiotêta?," p. 415.

[48] Cf. Feynman, *QED*.

[49] Rae, *Quantum Physics*, p. 61.

[50] Davies, *God and the New Physics*, pp. 108-9.

[51] Rae, *Quantum Physics*, p. 66-7.

[52] Rae refers to the studies of the Nobel prize-winning neurophysiologist, Sir John Eccles, who on the basis of experimental research came to distinguish between brain functions and the "self" or the "self-conscious mind" which interacts decisively with the brain (cf. Rae, *Quantum Physics*, pp. 64-6). This Self ("nucleus" or "bearer" of subjective self-consciousness) is perceived scientifically like the electron: only as an *a posteriori* determining of actual relations. But the *a posteriori* determining does not diminish in the least the empirical certainty of its existence. See J.C. Eccles, *Facing Reality*, Roche-Springer 1973; Karl Popper and John Eccles, *The Self and its Brain*, Springer 1977.

[53] Rae, *Quantum Physics*, p. 67.

[54] Trachanas, "Tychê ê anagkaiotêta?," p. 416.

[55] Feynman, *QED*, pp. 84-5, cf. pp. 122-3.

[56] Barrow and Tipler, *Anthropic Cosmological Principle*, p. 505.

[57] Trachanas, "Tychê ê anagkaiotêta?," p. 383; Barrow and Tippler, *Anthropic Cosmological Principle*, pp. 4-5, 6, 16.

[58] Trachanas, "Tychê ê anagkaiotêta?," p. 392; Xanthopoulos, *Peri asterôn*, pp. 118-22.

[59] Oikonomou, *Physikê sêmera*, vol. 1, pp. 162, 164; Rae, *Quantum Physics*, pp. 13-14.

[60] Trachanas, "Tychê ê anagkaiotêta?" p. 383.

[61] Trachanas, "Tychê ê anagkaiotêta?" pp. 384-5; Xanthopoulos, *Peri asterôn*, p. 120; D. Kotsakes and G. Kontopoulos, *Kosmologia*, Athens, 1982, p. 282; M. Papagiannis, *Origin of Life*, Japan: Center of Academic Publications, ed. H. Noda, 1978, p. 575.

[62] Trachanas, "Tychê ê anagkaiotêta?" p. 385; cf. Davies, *God and the New Physics*.

[63] Xanthopoulos, *Peri asterôn*, p. 120; Kotsakes and Kontopoulos, *Kosmologia*, pp. 281-2; cf. Davies, *God and the New Physics*.
[64] Xanthopoulos, *Peri asterôn*, p. 120; Kotsakes and Kontopoulos, *Kosmologia*, pp. 282-3.
[65] Trachanas, "Tychê ê anagkaiotêta?" p. 388.
[66] Trachanas, "Tychê ê anagkaiotêta?" p. 388; see also Wichmann, *Quantum Physics* .
[67] Trachanas, "Tychê ê anagkaiotêta?" p. 389.
[68] Trachanas, "Tychê ê anagkaiotêta?" p. 391, see also pp. 389-90; Kotsakes and Kontopoulos, *Kosmologia*, pp. 283-4; Wichmann, *Quantum Physics*, pp. 424-5; Xanthopoulos, *Peri asterôn*, pp. 118-19; Feynman, *QED*.
[69] Trachanas, "Tychê ê anagkaiotêta?" p. 401-3; Wichmann, *Quantum Physics*, p. 414; Steven Weinberg, *The First Three Minutes*, New York: Basic Books 1993.
[70] Hawking, *Brief History of Time*, pp. 140, 156.
[71] Trachanas, "Tychê ê anagkaiotêta?" p. 404-5: "The mass of our sun is around 2.10^{33} gr. As for the universe, we suppose that its visible portion is a significant part of the whole, so that, in estimating its size, the observed mass can be taken as equivalent to the whole."
[72] pp. 67-8.
[73] The expression is that of Jacques Lacan, *Le séminaire* XI, pp. 172, 180-1; see also Christos Yannaras, *Orthos logos kai koinônikê praktikê*, Athens: Domos, 1990, pp. 154-5.
[74] Freud uses the term "nucleus" (*Kern*) of subjectivity and is followed by Lacan who uses it to affirm the non-meaning (*non-sens*) of this "nucleus." (*Le séminaire* XI, p. 226). It is described as "non-meaning" to prevent the signifier "nucleus" from being taken as an ontological definition of what is signified. The nucleus of the subject (the subject's *hypostasis*) is marked out as non-meaning (*non-sens*) not because it really is nonexistent, but because it must be distinguished from any ontological meaning, since it can only be approached in terms of our mental processes.
[75] *Corpus Dionysiacum, On the Divine Names* 4.7, Migne, PG 3 701C.
[76] See Paul Davies, *God and the New Physics*, pp. 111-13. The physicist J. A. Wheeler maintains that the precise nature of reality awaits the active participation of a conscious observer. Thus the mind becomes responsible for the retrospective creation of reality – even if this reality existed before humankind. Cf. J.A. Wheeler, "Genesis and Observership," in R.E. Butts and J. Hintikka (eds), *Foundational Problems in the Special Sciences*, Reidel-Dordrecht 1977, p. 17.

Thesis 2

[1] Aristotle, *Generation of Animals* 1, 715b14-16.
[2] Plato, *Epinomis* 987a6; *Laws* 3, 676a8-b4.
[3] Aristotle, *Physics* 8, 263a14-15.
[4] Plato, *Parmenides* 145a3.
[5] Aristotle, *Metaphysics* 2, 994b30; *Physics* 3, 207a33-4.
[6] Aristotle, *Physics* 8, 263a14.
[7] *Politics* 2.7, 1267b3-4.
[8] *Laws* 1, 910b3-4.
[9] *Frgm.* 130,8.
[10] A preliminary outline of the problem, with references to the relevant psychoanalytical literature, is given in my book, *Orthos logos kai koinônikê praktikê*, IV, 2.
[11] For a representative example – amongst many other things – of dependence on the logic and argumentation of materialistic positivism see P. Kondyles, *Ischys kai apophasê: Hê diamorphôsê tôn kosmoeikonôn kai to problêma tôn axiôn*, Athens: Stigmi 1991.
[12] "Das Kunstwerk ist wohl ein angefertigtes Ding, aber es sagt noch etwas anderes, als das blosse Ding selbst ist, *allo agoreuei*:" *Holzwege*, Frankfurt: Klostermann 1963, p. 9.
[13] For a discussion of the semantics referring to the experience of *relationship* with what is signified see my *Prosôpo kai ho erôs*, section 67: "Eikonologikê glôssa: kôdikas anagnôseôs."
[14] Cf. the references to Einstein, Popper and Feyerabend in my *Orthos logos kai koinônikê praktikê*, p. 252ff.
[15] "One cannot, therefore, prove anything by crossing from another genus – e.g. something geometrical by arithmetic [...]. Arithmetical demonstrations always include the genus about which the demonstration is [...]. For this reason one cannot prove by geometry that there is a single science of opposites, nor even that two cubes make a cube; nor can one prove by any other science the theorems of a different one, except such as are so related to one another that the one is under the other – e.g. optics to geometry and harmonics to arithmetic:" Aristotle, *Posterior Analytics* I.7, 75a39-75b20 (trans. Jonathan Barnes).
[16] "Le sujet, *in initio*, commence au lieu de l'Autre, en tant que là surgit le premier signifiant:" Lacan, *Le séminaire* XI, p. 180.
[17] "*Desidero*, c'est le *cogito* freudien. C'est de là, nécessairement, qui s'institue l'essentiel du processus primaire:" Lacan, *Le séminaire* XI, p. 141.
[18] C'est la libido, en tant que pur instinct de vie c'est-à-dire de vie immortelle, de vie irrépressible, de vie qui n'a besoin, elle, d'aucun organe,

de vie simplifiée et indestructible:" Lacan, *Le séminaire* XI, p. 180.
[19] Denis Vasse, *Le temps du désir*, Paris: Seuil, p. 23; cf. pp. 34 and 40.
[20] Here with the psychoanalytical significance of the term. See Laplanche and Pontalis, *Vocabulaire de la psychanalyse*, p. 392 ff.

Thesis 3

[1] The relevant analyses of Lacan are revelatory with regard to the ontological problem. See my *Orthos logos kai koinônikê praktikê*, pp. 143-69, where there are references to the primary literature.
[2] Damascius, *On First Principles* 65 (ed. J. Kopp, Frankfurt 1826).
[3] "[...] isoler dans le sujet un coeur, un *kern*, pour s'exprimer comme Freud, de *non-sens*, que l'interprétation est elle-même un non-sens:" Lacan, *Le séminaire* XI, p. 226.
[4] Wittgenstein, *Tractatus* 3.3, 3.4, 3.42.
[5] See *Tractatus* 4.021, 4.022: "And I understand the proposition without having had its sense explained to me." "A proposition *shows* its sense" (trans. Pears-McGuinness).
[6] *Corpus Dionysiacum, On the Divine Names* 5.9, Migne, PG 3, 825A.
[7] *Tractatus* 4.0031 (trans. Pears-McGuinness).

Index